INTARSIA
Woodworking

MADE EASY

11 Projects to Build Your Skills

FOX CHAPEL
PUBLISHING

I would like to dedicate this book to my peers, the many intarsia friends I've met over the years, both virtually and in person. When I first began this journey, I had no idea that I would soon meet so many people with a shared passion for this amazing art form. Everyone was so welcoming and happily shared their knowledge. You helped me to find my passion and purpose. For that, I am grateful.

Special thanks to: Bruce Worthington, my intarsia partner in crime for many years. You challenged me with your designs, which built my confidence. Louise Hood, for encouraging me when I was just getting started. The late Charlie Norris, for helping and encouraging me to grow and nurture my art form. My customers, who thought my work was worth buying—especially those who trusted me to memorialize their precious furry loved ones. Kevin, my husband, who puts up with my wood addiction and messy shop, and provides honest feedback on my projects and designs. Marina Joseph, my best friend since high school. Your insight and wisdom helped me navigate the waters. Your reasoning kept me calm and focused. Your friendship keeps me grounded.

—Janette

Managing Editor: Gretchen Bacon
Acquisitions Editor: Kaylee J. Schofield
Editor: Joseph Borden
Designer: Joe Rasemas
Proofreader/Indexer: Jean Bissell

ISBN: 978-1-4971-0298-9

The Cataloging-in-Publication Data is on file with the Library of Congress.

To learn more about the other great books from Fox Chapel Publishing, or to find a retailer near you, call toll-free 800-457-9112 or visit us at *www.FoxChapelPublishing.com*.

We are always looking for talented authors. To submit an idea, please send a brief inquiry to acquisitions@foxchapelpublishing.com.

Printed in China
First printing

The art of intarsia has been rapidly gaining popularity among scroll saw artists and hobbyists over the last few years. The desire to learn something new and improve upon existing skills has never been greater. This book will become your go-to reference for mastering your skills. Don't be intimidated! Practice and patience go a long way in learning any new skill.

This book is full of new and fresh projects. It is geared toward all skill levels, and there is useful information for both beginners and seasoned enthusiasts. I will share with you what I have learned over more than 20 years of designing and creating intarsia. You will pick up new skills and refine existing ones to incorporate into your work. Whether you're brand new or well-seasoned, my goal is to showcase projects that will enhance and advance your artistic and technical abilities.

With each project, I incorporate skill-building lessons and techniques for you to practice and hone. As you work through each, you will build your skills incrementally.

The Getting Started section is for those new to the craft. It explains what you need to begin your journey into the wonderful world of intarsia. I will then take you through the primary steps I follow for each project in the Basic Steps of Intarsia section. It will help you to build your own basic "go-to" method that works best for you.

The Shaping Tips and Finishing Touches sections provide guidance and ideas to transform your craft into art! As with all art forms, everyone has their own unique style. To develop this, you first learn the basic techniques, master them, then incorporate them into your own work. As they say, you first learn the rules so you can decide which ones to break!

The project lessons are broken down into easy-to-follow segments with tips and instructions. Each project will highlight new techniques and incorporate previous ones. Beginner, intermediate, and advanced sections allow you to gradually build your skills and confidence. As you progress, more complex skills are incorporated into the advanced projects.

Early on in my intarsia journey, at my very first craft show, I met a wonderful intarsia artist named Charlie Norris. "How do you create those beautiful, complex pieces?" I asked. He replied, "The same way you create the easy ones: one piece at a time". To this day, I tell myself this simple yet profound message every time I begin a new project.

Table of Contents

54

76

70

38

96

28

Learning any new skill or craft can be intimidating, and intarsia is no exception. This book will help to conquer any fears you may have. It's not as difficult as it might seem—and the best part is, if you mess up a piece, you simply cut another. A minor mishap won't ruin an entire project like it can with other types of scroll sawing. When learning anything new, learn, practice, and learn some more. Each project in this book will take you a step further toward mastering the art.

Safety

While scroll sawing is pretty safe compared to many woodworking hobbies, there are still things to keep in mind before heading out to the shop. Not adhering to accepted safe practices can lead to serious injury. Keep these tips in mind each time you start a new project.

As with any tools, it's important to read all the manufacturer's instructions before use. A scroll saw is a fairly safe tool, but you can still hurt yourself. Always keep a firm grip on the piece and your fingers away from the blade when cutting. It's easy for the blade to get caught up in the wood while you cut, which can lead to kickback. I've had the wood "jump" before, and when it comes down on your fingers, it really hurts!

While your needs might not call for a dust collection system as large as mine, every woodworking shop should use a dust collection system of some sort—even if that's just a shop vacuum that connects to your powered tools to mitigate dust in the air.

Always use protective gear. Pictured here are some of the essentials: a respirator, several dust masks, rubber gloves, and safety glasses. The remote allows me to turn my dust collector on from a distance.

The greatest hazard with intarsia, as with any type of woodworking, is sawdust. Because there is so much sanding involved, and we often use many varieties of wood that can be hazardous to your health, it is imperative that adequate dust collection is used at all times. I also recommend wearing a quality dust mask, especially when shaping your work. For hand sanding and power carving, I created a downdraft table that hooks up to the dust collector.

When using any sanding tool, particularly one that spins, always be aware and careful while holding your work. I've had longer pieces kick back on me and, once, even rip my finger open. Keep your hair tied back and out of the way and don't wear loose-fitting clothing. And, while it might seem counter-intuitive, don't wear gloves while operating machinery, as they can get snagged in the moving parts.

When finishing your work, always have adequate ventilation, wear gloves, and wear safety glasses. Finish can easily splatter and get into your eyes. Be sure to dispose of used towels properly, as well. If left lying around, they can spontaneously combust, and that never ends well.

Enjoy your scrolling, but always be safe!

Ventilation, gloves, and safety glasses are essential when you're working with finishes.

Tools and Materials

To get started, you only need a few basic tools. As you progress, you can increase your arsenal as budget and space allow. When I first started intarsia, the only tools I had were a scroll saw, a drill press for sanding attachments, and a small shop vacuum. This is all you really need to get started. Over the years, I gradually added several sanding tools and a more efficient dust collector. You will likely already have many of these tools around your shop, but this list is handy if you're just setting up.

Scroll saw. If you don't already have a scroll saw, I suggest buying the best one you can afford. This is the main tool in your toolkit, and it will get a lot of use. If possible, it's always better if you have the option of trying it out beforehand to see how it runs and feels. At first, I purchased an inexpensive saw. It was okay to learn on initially, but it had a lot of vibration, and the blades were difficult to change. Overall, it wasn't a pleasant sawing experience. I ended up buying a higher-end saw soon after. My advice is to purchase a better saw to begin with. When cutting pieces for intarsia, you will be cutting thicker, and sometimes harder, woods than with other types of scroll work. If the experience isn't a pleasant one, it will discourage you from continuing. Everyone has their own opinion on which saw is the best. Do as much research as you can and ask other intarsia enthusiasts what works well for them. The best saw is the one you will use and enjoy!

Scroll saw blades. The type and size of scroll saw blade you use for intarsia varies depending on the type and thickness of wood you are cutting. Everyone has their own opinion as to the best blade to use. If you're new to scroll sawing, I suggest purchasing several sizes and styles of different brands. Test them, make notes, and try them with different woods to see what your preference is. Ultimately, you will settle on a favorite for most of your cutting.

Using the correct size and type of blade for intarsia can greatly improve your cutting experience. I see people struggle trying to cut a very hard, thick piece of wood with too fine a blade. A finer blade in intarsia does not necessarily mean more accuracy. If it takes you an hour and four blades to cut one piece, you will not enjoy the experience. An undersized blade will also potentially cause problems with the fit of your pieces. The blade can bow while cutting, causing the edges of the pieces to be uneven. It can also burn the wood.

In general, for cutting out most intarsia pieces, I prefer to use a higher-end #7 reverse tooth blade. Most of the wood you will be cutting is about ¾"–1" (1.9–2.5cm) thick. There are always exceptions, of course. For finer cuts on soft wood, a #5 would work well. For thick, exotic hardwood, a more aggressive blade would be better. The same blade number can vary with different brands and blade types. Some are more aggressive than others. I find Platinum OnLine #7 reverse tooth works well for me as an all-purpose blade for cutting intarsia. If I am cutting harder or thicker wood, or wood that burns easily, I will use a #7 Pegas Modified Geometry blade or a Flying Dutchman Polar blade. All are #7 but cut very differently.

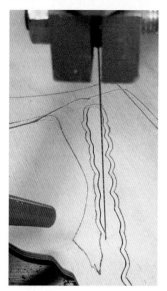

You also want to have finer blades on hand for different types of cutting. Backer boards for intarsia projects are thin, usually plywood that is ⅛"–¼" (3.2–6.4mm) thick. For this type of cutting, a fine blade such as a #2 or #2/0 works well. Using a higher number blade on such thin pieces will result in tear out and much less control over your cutting. When separating project pieces you've cut together (such as the rope in the Buoys on a Fence Post project), you will also need a finer blade. Depending on the thickness and type of wood, a #2, #3, or even #5 may be needed. You want the thinnest blade that will do the job well and without difficulty.

The most important thing about blades is to change them often. Blades can dull quickly. As soon as you notice yourself beginning to push the wood to cut it, it's time for a new blade. Cutting with a dull blade can result in cuts that aren't square, fatigue, frustration, and a poor fit. The life of blades can vary greatly depending on the wood you're cutting and the blade itself. Always let the blade do the work. If cutting is difficult, try using a different type of blade more suitable to what you are cutting. You should be steering the wood and holding it down, but not pushing it.

Sanders

Drill press with flex drum sander attachment (Option 1). I started with, and still use, flex drum sanders for most of my shaping. Flex drum sanders are simply dense foam wrapped in sandpaper of varying grits. They are inexpensive, work well, and can be attached to almost any motor that runs at about 1,725 rpm, which is the ideal speed for shaping intarsia pieces. At first, I used a drill press, interchanging grits as needed.

Sanding/buffing machine (Option 2). Eventually, I purchased a sanding/buffing tool that I can slide the flex drum sanders onto directly. I have a coarse-grit (80–120) on one side and a fine-grit (220) on the other. Bench grinders, lathes, and other motors can also be adapted for this purpose. You can purchase an arbor attachment for use on any of these. The key is to avoid anything that will spin too fast (over 2,000 rpm), or you will do more burning than sanding.

Inflatable drum sander (Option 3). An inflatable drum sander is another good option. This would be mounted in a similar manner as the flex drum sander. They are more expensive, but you don't need to replace them, just the sanding sleeve. You can also adjust the amount of air in them depending on your sanding needs. Inflatable drum sanders come in a variety of sizes, as well.

Oscillating spindle sander. An oscillating spindle sander is handy for adjusting minor fitting issues. You can remove small amounts of the edge of a piece for a better fit or square up the edge of a piece. The smallest spindle is a good option for this, whereas the larger spindles are great for removing a lot of wood at once. I use it often for shaping concave pieces, such as cat's ears. It is great for creating dips and curves to add dimension to a piece. Because it has a variety of spindle sizes, it is a versatile tool to have.

Rotary tool. A rotary tool with a flex shaft and assorted power carving bits is great for finer detail work or shaping small pieces. It also works well for getting into small areas. I use it a lot to rough in the overall shape of a project or an area within a project, such as an animal face—basically carving the general shape I'm trying to achieve, then using the flex drum sander to remove the scratches and fine-tune the individual pieces. It's important that the flex shaft is comfortable for you to hold. They come in varying sizes, so try it out ahead of time to ensure it will be comfortable in your hand.

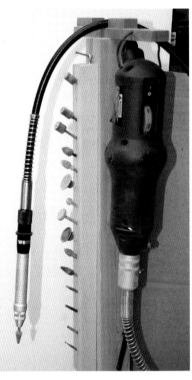

Mop sander. A sanding mop attachment is a must-have for my toolkit. As you will see in the project instructions, I utilize it to remove the "fuzzies" from the bottom of each piece. It is also used as the final sanding step to "buff" each piece to a smooth, soft finish. I use this sander on the drill press.

Belt sander. A belt sander is handy for flattening the bottom of the wood pieces before you begin cutting. It also works well for thinning pieces or removing a lot of wood. You can do some shaping with it as well, but it's not the ideal sander for this purpose.

Dust collection system. Sanding intarsia pieces creates a lot of fine sawdust. Some varieties of wood can be quite toxic. I highly recommend some sort of dust collection system, especially when you are shaping and sanding. There are many options available from homemade to commercial grade. A simple shop vac will do for starters. The downside is that you must reposition it for each tool you're using at the time, but it works well. If your budget allows, the ideal setup includes a proper dust collection unit with pipes, hoses, and gates going to the tools you use most.

Dust mask or respirator. Again, some woods can be highly toxic. Even for woods that are not, sawdust can wreak havoc on one's respiratory system. For these reasons, it is vital to invest in a good dust mask or respirator and get into the habit of wearing it whenever you are cutting or sanding.

Safety glasses. When working with wood and machinery, always wear shatterproof safety glasses to protect your eyes.

Square. A 2" (5.1cm) square is ideal for squaring your scroll saw blade.

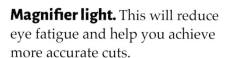

Magnifier light. This will reduce eye fatigue and help you achieve more accurate cuts.

Foot pedal for saw. This leaves both hands free to cut your pieces.

Clear packaging tape. This is placed on the wood before the pattern is adhered to it. It makes the pattern easy to remove and provides lubrication to your blade.

Spray adhesive. This is used to adhere pattern pieces.

Assortment of wood. The woods you will need will vary depending on your project and personal tastes.

Scissors. These are for cutting out patterns.

Sandpaper sheets. While you will do much sanding using powered sanders, you will need to hand sand at points.

Assorted clamps. These are mostly used for adhering the backer to the project.

Highlighter, black markers (both wide and thin), pencil, and eraser. These will be used for marking your patterns and wood pieces.

Two-sided turner's tape. This is used for adhering pieces to a sanding shim.

Blue painter's tape. This is used for protecting areas of wood for various reasons.

Wood glue. This is used for gluing your project together.

CA (cyanoacrylate) glue. This is a fast-acting glue that we will use to adhere various parts on some projects.

Waxed paper. You will often need to place your project on waxed paper so it does not stick to your work surface.

Awl. This is mostly used for tracing your project onto carbon/graphite paper.

Assorted drill bits. You will need several different sizes of drill bits for your projects.

Drill bit gauge. This will help determine what size drill bit you should use.

Dental tools, sharp-tipped and rubber-tipped. These are mostly used for cleaning wood finish out of hard-to-reach areas.

Wood Selection

This first step to creating an intarsia piece is an important one: selecting your wood. You can change the look of a project greatly just by the woods you choose for each piece. Try to maximize the use of color and grain in the wood to make the finished piece more interesting. Look at the pattern and photo of the project to help decide what type of wood and/or color would work best. I also like to find photographs of the subject I'm creating for additional ideas and reference. Once you've selected the wood, decide which direction the grain should go. Sometimes, the grain itself is more important than the actual color. I like to choose wood with interesting grains, particularly for areas such as water, rocks, or larger areas that will stand out and really highlight the personality of the wood.

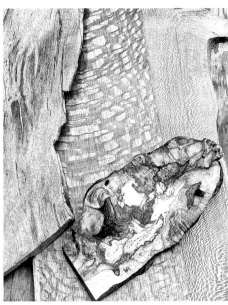

To give your project more depth, choose woods with interesting grain patterns.

By taking advantage of the wood grain, you can make a good project spectacular.

When you're just starting out and haven't yet accumulated many different types of wood, I suggest starting with domestic woods. They are more affordable and generally easier to work with, particularly soft woods. They can have some great grain patterns, as well. As you complete more projects and the need arises, you'll no doubt go on the hunt for certain colors or species. This is when the wood addiction begins! If you have a specific project that requires certain shades, buy a little extra to have on hand for that next project. You will accumulate a good variety in no time! Domestic and exotic woods come in just about every color imaginable. Be aware that with some species the colors may change over time, dramatically even. Take this into account when planning your project. If you're not sure, put the board in sunlight or a bright area, cover part of it from exposure to the light, and examine it over time to compare the exposed area with the covered area.

Generally, boards between ¾"–1" (1.9–2.5cm) thick are ideal for intarsia. Any thinner and you lose the three-dimensional appearance that intarsia is known for. Any thicker and cutting can become difficult with a scroll saw. You don't have to have every piece of a project the same thickness. Sometimes, you can only find certain types of wood as ⅞" (2.2cm) or ¹⁵⁄₁₆" (2.4cm), for example. Thickness can be reduced during the shaping process. Adding risers in strategic areas to make them thicker will also add dimension. The size of your overall project will factor in as well. Small projects, such as ornaments, don't need to be created with thicker woods, but a very large project would look flat if all the wood was thin.

TIP

One trip to the lumber store will reveal that there are many options. Something to keep in mind is that more common types of wood will often come in different forms. They can be anywhere from rough-sawn to planed and sanded on all sides. Generally, the less processing the mill has to do, the cheaper the board will be. Lumber also comes in different grades. The more defects in the board, the cheaper it will be. If you have the ability and don't mind doing some prep work, you can save quite a bit of money by purchasing less-processed lumber. When first starting out, I suggest getting S4S (sanded on four sides) to start with because it is easier to work. Since you're cutting small pieces out of a board, a lower-grade board may not be an issue and can save you some money. Keep in mind that there will be more waste. You will have to work around knots and other defects or incorporate them into your project. I tend to buy the board that has the most interesting grain in it, rather than straight, defect-free grain.

Most lumber stores don't require you to purchase the entire board of lumber as long as you leave a minimum based on their store policy, usually 6' (1.8cm) or so.

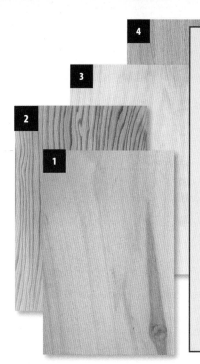

While your exact needs will depend on the project and the specific look you're trying to achieve, here's a guideline for some common woods used in intarsia. Availability varies regionally, so find what works best and is easily sourced in your area.

- Aspen (1), cedar (2), and maple (3) are great for lighter colors.
- Poplar (4) and sycamore (5) are good for medium/light colors.
- Lacewood (6) is great for texture such as scales.
- Use walnut (7) or similar for darker hues.
- Use redwood (8) or similar for reddish hues.

See the projects in this book for even more exotic woods that can elevate your work.

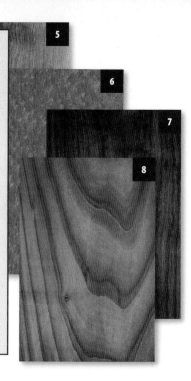

How to Read Intarsia Patterns

Reading intarsia patterns is pretty straightforward. Every designer has their own preference when it comes to the amount of information on a pattern. The pattern is basically an outline or line drawing of individual pieces that, once you copy the pattern, can be cut out and applied to the wood. Most designers will add lines to each pattern piece. These lines suggest the best direction the grain should go for the flow of the finished piece. There can be letters such as M or D to indicate a wood shade preference (medium or dark). Some patterns use other indicators to show you where it would be best to increase or decrease the thickness of the wood. Dashed lines can suggest areas to contour, options for leaving two pieces as one, or other texture methods. Because everyone has their own preferences regarding how much or how little information is on a pattern, you will find some differences between designers.

Look for a key or guide on the pattern to explain any symbols or letters. Patterns should come with a color photo of the completed project for reference purposes. This, in my opinion, is the most important tool for the person making the project. If there is extra space, additional instruction on the areas around the pattern is great to have. My preference is to not clutter up the space within the pieces themselves. It can get confusing with too much going on. I do apply directional lines and let the person making the project decide for themselves what markings, if any, they need. My intention is not to have someone "copy" the project as I made it, but to use their own imagination. One thing to note is that it's important to respect the copyright on any designer's pattern. Never share copies of patterns you have purchased with others. This violates the designer's copyright.

Key-suggestions only
L=Light
ML=Medium Light
MD=Medium Dark
D=Dark

You may make up to 10 copies of this pattern for your own personal use

This is what a typical key on an intarsia pattern might look like.

I do not expect people to do things exactly as I have done them, thus I usually only include directional lines on my patterns.

Intarsia patterns aren't the only things you can use for making intarsia pieces. Quilt patterns, stained glass patterns, or coloring book pages are great options, too. You may need to make some slight modifications, but these generally work well for intarsia.

LET'S GET STARTED!

In this section, I have listed the basic steps of intarsia projects to serve as a quick-start guide. You can refer to these steps as needed when completing the projects that follow. Each project also has added instruction and sometimes additional steps specifically pertaining to it. When first starting out, I recommend following each step exactly. Over time, you will develop your own routine and methods that work best for you.

INTARSIA OVERVIEW

1. Select wood and prepare the pattern
2. Adhere the pattern to the wood and prepare the wood for cutting
3. Cut out the pieces and remove the fuzzies
4. Remove the pattern, number the pieces, assemble the project, and correct fit issues
5. Shape the project
   - Rough shaping
   - Adding contouring
   - Smoothing the pieces
   - Fine tuning
6. Glue the project
7. Apply the finish
8. Make the backer board
9. Glue the project to the backer
10. Attach the hanger

Tracing Method vs. Cut-and-Paste Method

Once you decide on a project, you need to prepare the pattern for use. There are basically two methods to apply the pattern to the wood: draw onto the wood using tracing or graphite paper or adhere an actual copy of the pattern piece onto the wood.

Tracing method. Tracing the pattern has a few advantages. If you don't have access to a photocopier or printer, this would be the easiest method to use. It's not nearly as accurate as using a copy of the actual pattern, but it will work if done carefully. First, determine where you will cut the piece from the wood. Then, place the pattern on top of the wood. Holding one side of the pattern in place, slip the carbon or graphite paper underneath. Tape the pattern in place with painter's tape to prevent it from moving. Carefully trace the pattern onto the wood with a sharp pencil.

Several problems can arise with this method. It's easy for a project to become distorted and not fit well. It's difficult to see the lines when cutting dark wood such as walnut. Hand-drawn lines can be difficult to follow, especially if traced over unsanded or rough wood.

Cut-and-paste method. My preferred method is the cut-and-paste method. I have found the easiest and most accurate way is to make multiple copies of the pattern, then cut out individual pattern pieces to attach to the wood.

Step One: Prepare the Pattern

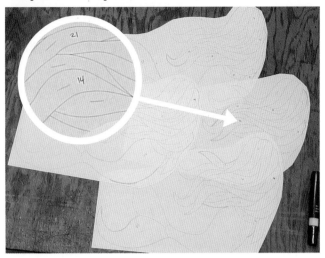

Number the pieces on your master pattern to make them easy to identify later as you cut.

Number the pieces on the master pattern. Have five or six copies of the pattern on hand (the actual number of copies you need depends on the pattern itself and how you number the pieces on them). Number each piece on the cut-out pages so no adjoining piece is already numbered unless you plan to cut the two pieces out together.

With a yellow highlighter, mark the outer edge of the numbered pieces prior to cutting them. This is optional, but it helps to remind you where the outside edge is so you can relax your cutting.

Step Two: Cut Out and Adhere the Pattern Pieces

For small projects, it's easiest to cut out all the pattern pieces at once. For larger projects, it is easier to cut pieces out in groupings according to wood type or particular sections.

Make alignment markings on your pattern piece and the wood so the pattern can be perfectly realigned after you apply the adhesive.

Whether you choose to cut all the pieces out at once or in segments (such as by wood variety or areas of a pattern) is up to you. For me, it depends on the size of the project and number of pieces. On a smaller project, it's generally easier to cut out all the pieces at once, then group them according to wood type or color. If the project is larger or more detailed, it's easier to cut pieces out in sections, either by wood variety or area of the project you want to work on first.

Select the wood you're going to use and apply clear packaging tape to the wood. This does two things: it helps to lubricate the blade as you cut, and it makes pattern removal easy afterward. It peels off without leaving any residue. Clear tape also allows you to see the wood grain, which helps when placing your pattern piece. This way, you can be sure you're taking full advantage of the grain for your project.

After you've applied the tape, dry-fit the pattern pieces onto the wood. Take the grain and its direction into consideration. When wood options are limited, I will place alignment marks going from the edge of the pattern on to the tape for each piece so it can be realigned exactly where I want it to go once the adhesive is applied. If you have several adjoining pattern pieces that are the same color and grain direction, you can usually cut these pieces out together, then separate them later.

Finally, apply a light coat of temporary bond spray adhesive to the back of the pattern piece. Then, apply the pattern piece to the clear packaging tape.

Step Three: Cut the Wood

Use a belt sander to remove any extra material so your workpiece is level and flat.

Once the pattern pieces are attached, cut the pieces of wood into manageable sizes before cutting out the individual pieces. You should be able to easily maneuver the piece around the scroll saw table while cutting. Make sure the bottom of the piece is flat and doesn't rock back and forth. If it isn't flat, your cuts may not be square. Use a belt sander to sand the piece flat, if needed.

Rub the scroll saw blade with high-grit sandpaper to remove any oil so it doesn't slip while you are working.

Before you do any cutting, you'll need to prepare your blade. Always start a project with a new blade. Gently rub either end of the new blade with fine-grit sandpaper. This will remove any oil residue and help to prevent the blade from slipping.

It's a good idea to get into the habit of checking that the blade is square to the table before you begin. There

Place a small square against your blade and check for gaps to determine if it is square.

Check your blade's squareness by cutting into a scrap piece of wood. Then, remove the wood and place it behind the blade. You should be able to easily fit the blade into the cut you just made.

If you cut a corner off a piece of scrap wood and there are gaps when you place a square against the wood, your blade is not square.

are several ways to check this. The easiest is to place a small square beside the tightened blade. The blade should run parallel to the square with no gaps. If it isn't square, adjust the top or bottom of the blade until it's parallel from top to bottom.

Another way to test the squareness of the blade is to make a cut into a scrap piece of wood that is ¾"–1" (1.9–2.5cm) thick. Place the wood behind the blade and see if it easily goes into the cut you just made. You can also cut off the corner of a piece of scrap wood and hold the square against it. A gap on the top or bottom of the wood will indicate adjustments need to be made.

A square blade and accurate cutting are the keys to a good fit when cutting out intarsia pieces. Never force the blade. Guide it along the pattern line with light, even pressure. As soon as you notice yourself pushing harder, it's time to change the blade. Forcing a dull blade through the wood will cause it to flex, which will result in a cut that is not square.

Of course, having a sharp and square blade is only the first step to cutting well. When you're cutting pieces for intarsia patterns, keep these tips in mind:

- Be consistent with your cutting. If you cut down the center of the line, continue this for every piece.

- When you come to a tight turn, complete it in multiple passes. Never force a sharp turn around a curve. Go beyond the line, then back up, and cut out a small hole in the waste section of the wood. This will keep the blade from twisting and gives it space to turn. Continue around the corner, nibbling away until the turn is completed.

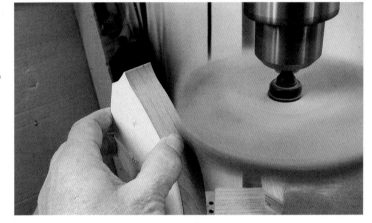

- When cutting wood that is thick or very hard, go slow or switch to a larger blade. Resist the urge to force the blade through the wood. In addition to leading to poor results, forcing a blade can cause it to overheat or warp, which can lead to injury and breakage.

Once the pieces are all cut, remove any fuzzies from the bottom of each piece. This is most easily done with a sanding mop. A light touch should remove them. Sanding by hand also works well. If left on, fuzzies can affect the fit of the pieces.

Cutting wood will leave behind "fuzzies." Remove these to ensure a good fit for your intarsia project.

Step Four: Remove the Pattern, Number the Pieces, and Assemble

Transfer the piece number to the bottom of the piece and remove the pattern. This helps you keep track of where they belong. It also helps you to avoid accidentally shaping the wrong side of the piece. Then, assemble the pieces onto the master copy of the pattern. This gives you your first view of how the project will look when finished. If there are any pieces that don't look right based on the wood you selected, now is the time to recut that piece.

After removing the pattern from the wood, transfer the pattern piece number onto the cutout.

This is also the time you should correct any fit issues. Small gaps can seem like huge, gaping spaces that you only see once the project is assembled. For the artist, a gap may seem to be 1" (2.5cm) wide, when in reality it's probably less than ⅟₃₂" (0.8mm). There is no general rule of "acceptable" width for gaps between pieces. You, as the artist, must decide how well the pieces need to fit. We are always our own worst critic, and chances are it's not as big as you think it is. The same size gap will seem much larger on a smaller project than it will on a large piece. That said, there are steps you can take to correct most minor fit issues.

In the picture above, you'll notice a variety of gaps, both large and small. As the artist, you must decide if the gaps are acceptable and, if not, correct any issues.

Use a spindle sander to address any problem areas to ensure a good fit.

The first thing is to make sure all the fuzzies on the bottom of the piece have been removed. They can show up on corners or edges as well, particularly on soft woods such as pine. Then, hold the pieces together where the gap is to determine what part of the edge is creating the problem. There is usually a slight bump where you may have strayed off the line slightly. Using an oscillating spindle sander with an appropriately sized spindle attached, gently go over just the problem area. Remove a very small amount of material at a time and recheck the fit often. Drawing a pencil line on the edge that needs adjustment is helpful. If the fit issue is not reachable by a spindle sander, you can use a scroll saw blade to shave off some of the area that needs trimming. Again, only remove a small bit of material at a time.

For fit issues with points fitting into *V* cuts, try sanding the point slightly with a block and sandpaper. You can also deepen the *V* slightly with your scroll saw blade. For curves, the problem is usually that the curve isn't square. The blade might have flexed during cutting. Go over this area with the spindle sander, repeating as necessary until the curved pieces fit together.

Step Five: Shape the Project

Shaping is the most important part of intarsia. This is where the artistry really comes into play. Like any art form, everyone has their own style. You spend so much time creating a project; this is not the place to skimp to save time. Because of its importance, I have dedicated an entire section to shaping where I go into more detail and provide useful tips (see Introduction to Shaping on page 22). Each project in this book also has its own shaping information to guide you.

The basic shaping steps are:

- **Rough shaping.** Create the general overall shape of the project.

- **Smooth shaping.** Go over each piece, removing scratches and making minor adjustments.

- **Detail sanding.** Soften edges, make minor adjustments so the pieces flow together, and remove any pencil marks.

- **Final sanding or buffing.** Go over each piece with a sanding mop to soften and buff.

A flame-point burr is excellent for removing material quickly.

Step Six: Glue the Project.

There are several ways to glue your project together. Some prefer to glue the individual pieces directly to the backer, either before or after applying finish. After trying this method, I found several problems can arise. The first is aligning everything perfectly so that no part of the backer shows once the pieces have been glued. There's no easy way to correct this after the glue dries other than hand sanding the visible part of the backing. There also isn't as much strength to the overall project with this method.

I prefer to edge glue all the pieces together prior to finishing. The glue adheres better to bare wood than to wood with finish applied. Begin by putting a sheet of waxed paper over the master pattern, then assemble the project on top. Depending on the complexity of your project, gluing can be tricky because pieces can easily shift during this process.

I prefer yellow wood glue for most projects. Squeeze a small amount into a tin can and apply to the lower half of the edge to be glued. A skewer is handy for this purpose. When the skewer develops too much dried glue on the end, you can easily shave it off with a utility knife. If you have a critical area that needs to bond quickly, add a few dots of CA (cyanoacrylate) gel glue in addition to the wood glue. It will act as the clamp while the stronger wood glue dries.

Begin by gluing small segments together (an eye and pupil, flower petals, feather areas, etc.). Always reinsert these segments back into the main project to ensure everything continues to fit the way it should. Next, apply glue to the piece sitting on the waxed paper, then insert or set the adjoining piece next to it. A thin line of glue is all you need. Continually reassemble the entire project and keep checking the fit as you go to ensure that nothing shifts.

For large projects, it's best to glue in sections. Select a dividing point that has the least number of adjoining pieces. Glue the first segment together. Create multiple segments, then glue all the segments together. With these large projects, it can be easier to complete the final glue up of the larger segments after the finish has been applied.

For any project, always allow the glue to dry thoroughly before applying finish.

Use a skewer to apply wood glue to the lower edge of your workpiece.

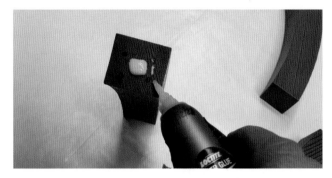

Apply a bit of CA glue to create a tighter bond while the wood glue dries.

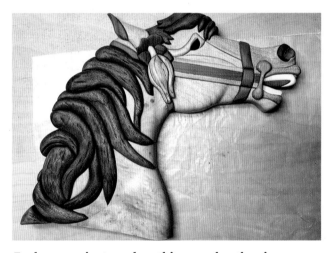

For large projects such as this one, glue the pieces in sections. For instance, you might start with the mane here.

Step Seven: Apply Finish

There are different types of finishes and methods you can use for finishing your intarsia project. I suggest trying different methods until you find one that works best for you. Everyone has their own preferences. I don't recommend using a glossy spray finish. First, the gloss makes the project look too shiny, which, to me, detracts from the overall look. It's difficult to evenly coat with a spray when there are so many angles and crevices to get into. There are also the fumes to consider, unless you have good ventilation. Danish oil and other liquid finishes work well. I have used these on projects that are delicate or have rough surfaces.

The drawback I have found with Danish oil is that the odor lingers for a while. Avoid any finishes that require sanding between coats unless you plan to finish the individual pieces before gluing them together.

I use a clear satin gel varnish to finish intarsia projects. Bartley's Gel Varnish and Old Masters Gel Polyurethane are two excellent choices. It takes a bit of extra work, but the results are worth the effort. They leave a nice, soft sheen to the wood. You don't have to worry about dust or sanding between coats, and they are easy to work with. Overall, they are very forgiving about dust or sanding between coats, and they are easy to work with.

Use a small brush to apply varnish to your project.

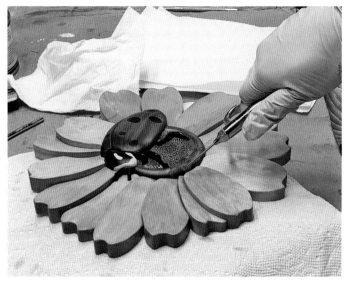

Use an air compressor to blow excess finish out of the project's cracks.

Apply a generous amount of gel varnish to the project. Begin with the edges and work your way around, getting into all the nooks and crannies. Soft woods will absorb the finish faster than hardwoods. If this happens, apply additional finish for it to soak up. Wipe off as much excess as possible with paper towels.

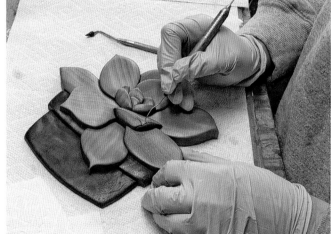

Use a combination of a rubber-tipped dental tool, a sharp dental tool, and a paper towel to get finish out of hard-to-reach areas.

Gently blow excess finish out of the cracks with an air compressor, covering the area in front of it to avoid excess splatter around the shop. Always wear safety glasses for this step. Next, wipe off any excess, then go around each piece with a paper towel and a rubber-tipped dental tool, getting excess out of the hard-to-reach areas. The sharp dental tool works great for getting stubborn or dried finish out of the cracks, as well as removing any from kerf lines. As you find finish in cracks, blow it out and continue. Finally, go over the entire project with clean paper towels. Hold the piece up to the light at different angles to ensure all has been removed. Apply a minimum of two coats of finish, allowing the piece to dry thoroughly between each.

Step Eight: Make the Backer

A backer is recommended to add additional strength to a project. It provides a clean and neat professional-looking appearance, as well. The backer hides the risers, glue, and other unsightly markings usually found on the back of a project. It also gives you a clean place to list your woods and sign your piece. Overall, it adds a finished look to the project.

I recommend using quality plywood for the backing. My preference is ⅛" (3.2mm) Baltic or Finnish birch. For larger or more fragile projects, I recommend ¼" (6.4mm) board. Other materials to consider include hardboard, Masonite, or lauan plywood. You want something that has at least one good side that will show on the back and is strong enough to add support to the finished project.

Step Nine: Affix the Project to the Backer

The first step is to trace the finished project onto the plywood. If there are any tight areas that a pencil won't fit into, use carbon or graphite paper. Slip the paper under the project and use an awl or other sharp tool to trace where the pencil won't reach.

Next, use a fine #2 or #3 reverse tooth blade to cut out the backer. Cut approximately ⅛" (3.2mm) inside the traced line. You don't want the backer to be visible when the piece is hanging on the wall. Then, sand the edges and back of your backing for an extra professional touch.

With the exceptions of projects that are primarily light in color, I darken the edges with a black, wide-tip permanent marker. This makes the backer less noticeable once your project is displayed on a wall. As a bonus, I always list the woods used on the back of the project. Each piece is also numbered and signed.

Next, apply a thin coat of wood glue to the "up" side of the backer with a disposable glue or foam brush. Work quickly, spreading the glue right to the edges. Avoid leaving excess amounts of glue an any areas or it could potentially squeeze through to the front of the piece. Then, place the project face down on a protected surface. Apply the backer and wiggle it around to ensure good glue contact. Check the entire perimeter to make sure that the backer is centered and not visible from the front.

An awl or other sharp tool is ideal for tracing onto the backer board where a pencil won't reach.

Go over the edges of the backer with a black permanent marker to give it a more polished look.

Spread a thin coat of wood glue on your backer, taking care not to use too much so it doesn't come through the front of the project.

Apply as many clamps as needed to ensure complete contact. Use soft cloths or old socks to protect the face of the project from being marked by the clamps. You can never use too many clamps! Where clamps aren't practical, such as on large projects, flip the project right side up, protect the surface, and apply sandbags or other heavy, non-sharp items on top. Remove any excess glue that squeezes out around the edges with an awl or paper towel.

Clamp the project to the backer, using as many clamps as you need to ensure a tight bond.

Step Ten: Attach the Hanger

There are many types of hangers. Depending on the size of your project, you will need to make sure that whatever you use is rated for the project's weight. To determine where your hanging point should be, balance the project between your thumb and forefinger, adjusting until it hangs at the desired angle. Put a pencil mark at the balance spot. Check to ensure that the screw to attach the hanger isn't longer than the thickness of the project and backer. Make an indent on the pencil mark with an awl. This helps keep the screw from wandering. Screw the hanger in place.

For larger projects, a heavy-duty hanger will be necessary. Depending on the shape, sometimes it is easiest to mount screws or hangers on either side and attach picture wire. Make sure the hook you attach to the wall is also rated for the weight of your piece. If you find that the piece doesn't hang quite straight, or the top sits farther from the wall

The type of hanger you need will depend on the size and shape of your project. Be sure to check that whatever hanger you use is rated for the project's weight.

than the bottom, apply rubber bumpers to two spots on the bottom. These bumpers stick to the wall, keeping the project in place.

Developing your own process and style takes time. Once you master the basics, you may modify them or find different techniques that work best for you. Now to make some sawdust!

Introduction to Shaping

Shaping is the essence of intarsia. This is where the artistry really comes into play. Like any art form, everyone has their own style. There is no right or wrong way to shape intarsia pieces; however, by following some basic guidelines initially, you will discover which techniques work best for you. The finished project is a work of art that should reflect your own style.

When shaping, think of yourself as a sculptor. You are attempting to create the illusion of a three-dimensional work of art in a two-dimensional medium.

There are basically four steps to the shaping process:

- **Rough shaping,** to get the general overall shape of your pieces.

- **Smooth shaping,** where you go over each piece, removing all scratches and fine tuning any places that might need adjustment, adding continuity to the overall piece.

- **Hand/detail sanding,** which softens edges and helps each piece better align with other pieces. This is also a good time to remove any pencil lines and fuzzies on the bottom of the pieces.

- **Finish sanding, where you go over the project with a final fine sanding.** For this step, I use a sanding mop.

This piece creates depth by utilizing varying wood thicknesses and using contouring to create an impression of movement. This project uses green poplar, yellowheart, redwood, maple, blue pine, aspen, red cedar, walnut, and red sycamore.

Getting Perspective

While it is not absolutely necessary to go through each of these steps, spending the time doing so will result in a nicer-looking project. I have provided you with shaping guidance for each project throughout this book. These tips can be applied to future projects, too.

There are many different sanding and shaping tools available. I've gone over some of the essentials in the Getting Started section. My go-to sanding tool is the flex drum sander. More and more, I find that I am also making use of the rotary tool and power carving burrs. Needle files and hand sanding are great for small areas and fine tuning. The oscillating spindle sander has become a must-have for roughing out pieces and correcting minor fit issues. Whatever you have available is the best tool to have.

Before you begin shaping, it is important to study your project. Try to envision what it would look like if it were three-dimensional. If your project is an animal, study photographs of that animal from different angles. Referring to your project, decide which areas should appear farther away or closer. A basic rule of thumb is that thicker wood represents the appearance of being closer to the viewer and thinner wood represents farther away. I spend a great deal of time thinking about how a project will be shaped. What needs to stand out farther? What should taper off and blend into the adjoining pieces? What do you want to emphasize as the focal point? Some pieces will flow and blend into each other, and some will stand out.

In this example, the lighthouse building on the left is "closest" to the viewer, while the clouds and sky are off in the distance. This project is the perfect example of perspective being utilized in intarsia. The near and distant elements, the angle the lighthouse is being viewed from, and the contouring of the foreground add movement and interest. By making the lighthouse from thicker wood, or adding risers to the pieces, you give the illusion that it is closer to the viewer. When shaped, it needs to stand out as the focal point. The green mountain area "in front" of the lighthouse is higher and the edges are rounded to meet the edge of the water.

When shaping an animal, envision how the individual pieces relate to the pieces around them, how they should flow together or stand apart. In intarsia, you're after the illusion of a three-dimensional piece. In this example, the collie's head is turned to the left. The left side of the head is "behind" or farther away from the viewer than the muzzle. To give this illusion, the pieces on the left are lowered and risers are added to the muzzle to raise it even higher. Once the muzzle area was raised, it had to be shaped on a downward slope to meet up with the top of the head pieces above it. These pieces were blended to give the impression of a sloped forehead. Notice how the left front leg is raised to appear closer, then rounded down to meet the rest of the body. It stands out from the fur. To give the appearance of fluffiness or long hair, the fur pieces were shaped so they are thinner at the top. This causes the bottom of the pieces above them to seem higher. They are also contoured to give the sense that the dog is sitting outside on a windy day.

This project uses many sloped and rounded pieces, among other techniques, to give the dog a three-dimensional look.

Note how the car seems to jump out at the viewer, though it is constructed on a nearly flat surface. This project uses curly maple, mahogany, hackberry, buckeye burl, ebony, cherry, red cedar, Peruvian walnut, and aspen.

I use the term "illusion" a lot. Intarsia became a true art form not long after perspective (in the artistic sense) was discovered. By making use of perspective, artisans can give the illusion of something more dimensional than it actually is. Perspective plays a big role in intarsia, especially in larger projects. You are trying to give the appearance of something that has much greater depth than its 1"–2" (2.5–5.1cm) thickness.

Shaping Techniques

For me, starting the shaping process is the hardest part. *Where do I begin? How thin or thick should I go?* I still find these questions difficult on some projects. It's best to do a small amount at a time and gradually proceed until things fall into place.

Envision your project three-dimensionally, mentally planning what areas should appear closer to you or farther away. Some people find starting at what will end up as the lowest or thinnest point and working their way "up" in thickness works best. Others start at the highest point and work their way to thinner areas. Some like to work from top to bottom or vice versa. If I get stumped, I'll start at the easiest or most obvious point and work from there. There isn't any correct starting point except what works best for you. I will frequently jump around to different areas until everything falls into place.

You will see many different shaping techniques demonstrated throughout this book. Each project provides valuable information to build your skills and help to develop your own unique style. For each piece of artwork that you create, try to add a little something extra to make it better than the last. Don't be afraid to try new techniques and experiment.

Creating Depth and Contours

Areas that you want to appear farther away or in the background should be thinned down. This can be done through sanding an individual piece or cutting the wood thinner to begin with. Varying the thickness throughout the project adds visual interest and variety to a finished piece.

Adding risers is the easiest way to increase the thickness of a piece. Risers are simply scrap pieces of wood used to elevate specific areas or individual pieces within the project. Most of the wood used in intarsia is about ¾"–1" (1.9–2.5cm) thick. Any thicker and it would be difficult to cut with a scroll saw, not to mention the cost of the wood itself. Any type of wood will work for risers, but plywood tends to be more stable and uniform in thickness. The only limit to the thickness you can use is the surrounding pieces. You never want to go higher than the lowest adjacent piece. Otherwise, you will create an unsightly gap. Always leave at least ⅛" (3.2mm) overlap beside an adjoining piece. You also don't want risers to be visible on an outside edge. If you need to increase the thickness on an edge piece, it's best to utilize the same wood as the piece itself and glue two pieces together

Adding contour to an individual piece or multiple pieces creates added interest and realism. It's an important piece of the puzzle. Curving a leaf, for example, or tapering one side of a flower petal lower, or adding dips and waves to water gives an impression of movement and flow. Taking the time to add these details will elevate your work. Subtle nuances will draw the viewer's attention and make your work stand out. In this example of the carousel horse legs, I spent a great deal of time and used multiple methods to create the muscle tone in the carousel horse's legs and body. Many different tools were utilized for shaping this project, including multiple types of carving burrs and files. It can seem daunting, but if you work on one piece at a time, it will be done before you know it!

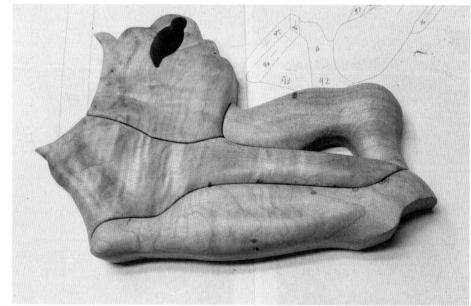

Adding contour to a project helps to create movement and a sense of realism.

Shaping Pieces

Plan what areas of a project can be shaped together as "one" piece and what pieces should be shaped individually. Not every piece needs to be rounded over. Something I see from some beginners is what I call "bubble shaping" where every single piece has rounded edges whether they should be in "reality" or not.

Let's look at the two larger fish in this project as an example. They both have multiple pieces in the main body. Rather than shape each body piece individually, I've shaped them together, as if they were all one piece. It creates a smoother and more realistic look than if each piece had been shaped individually. To do this, you can either glue the pieces together prior to shaping, or use a sanding shim.

Sometimes it is best to shape pieces together instead of individually for a more realistic look. This project uses lacewood, sycamore, red cedar, walnut, maple, red alder, butternut, and Peruvian walnut.

A sanding shim is nothing more than scrap plywood cut roughly the same size and shape as the pieces you want to shape together. Use double-sided tape to attach the pieces to the shim and sand them as you would if they were one piece. This creates a continuity of shape throughout. Plywood that is a minimum of ¼" (6.4mm) thick works best for sanding shims.

When I create a portrait of an animal, I will usually begin by assembling the entire face onto a piece of ½" plywood. To get an idea of how I want to proceed, I will start with a rotary tool and carve strategic areas until I get the rough shape I'm looking for. From here, I can move on to the individual pieces and refine the shape as I go.

When shaping pieces individually, begin gradually. You can go back and remove more material, but you can't put it back once it's gone. It's important to shape each piece so that it looks natural when compared to the pieces around it. If you do find that you've gone too far, you may be able to add a riser to the piece to bring it up higher, then reshape it.

Whether individual pieces are cut to represent a separate area or different-colored shading of the same area on a project, how you shape them can greatly affect the overall look of the finished project. As you shape each piece, it is important to consider all the pieces and how they relate to each other. If you do this, your overall finished product will have a more natural and cohesive look.

As with any style of art, time and practice are key to developing and refining your own unique style.

Use a rotary tool to carve out the rough shape you're hoping to achieve before moving to individual pieces.

Finishing Touches

The way a project is completed, and the extra time spent at the final stages, can turn an ordinary project into a spectacular one. I have seen projects where the cutting and shaping were exceptional, only to see shortcuts on the finish or some other small detail. Here are a few added ideas to further enhance your projects.

Adding Texture

Sometimes you might find that adding texture to certain parts of a project can enhance the overall look. There are many ways to do this. There is no right or wrong method. Use your imagination to come up with whatever works best to achieve the look you are aiming for.

Using a rotary tool and power carving bits is an easy and effective way to add texture to a project. Depending on the bit you select, many different effects can be achieved. It's always best to practice on scrap pieces of the same type of wood you plan to texture to ensure that the results fit the look you are after.

Another tool that can be useful for texturing is a Wonder Wheel, which is an abrasive wheel you can attach to your grinder. Wire brushes (either handheld or mounted in a drill press) can also be useful.

Sometimes distressing a piece of wood can help to achieve a weather-beaten look. After shaping, I sometimes add extra gouges and marks. It goes against my nature to rough them up this way because my brain says, "Make it smooth!" but I force myself and I am always pleased with the results. I've used hammers, gouges, and the spindle sander to distress these pieces.

Creating intentional imperfections by marring the wood's surface is a great way to give your project an aged look.

A rotary tool and various bits are essential to adding texture to a finished intarsia project.

TIP If the wood is overly spalted, you can stabilize it with CA glue after shaping.

Utilizing "less-than-perfect" wood is a great way to add an interesting aesthetic to the project. When I make small birds, I like to have them sitting on something. I select pieces of wood for the tree or branch that may otherwise be unusable, such as the end of the log with the bark still on, spalted pieces, or anything that will make the project more interesting. I keep a bin full of many unique pieces of wood for this purpose.

After adding texture to my pieces, I go over them lightly with the sanding mop. This gives them a more consistent look with the rest of the pieces.

This project uses wood that has considerable spalting to achieve a dynamic look.

If you need to achieve a unique effect, such as adding color to eyes, there's nothing wrong with using watercolors or similar paints.

Adding Color

Add color to intarsia? Aren't you supposed to do that by using different woods? Well, most of the time, yes. Sometimes adding color is the only way to achieve the look you want—and there is nothing wrong with that. There are many ways to add color. Generally, I prefer to use natural wood colors whenever possible. Sometimes, wood just doesn't come in the color you need, or it's not available to you. I have made several custom Ragdoll cat portraits over the years. Their eyes are always beautiful shades of blue. To make the project more realistic, I use a watercolor wash to color the eyes. By mixing shades of blue and white and varying the amount of water, I try to match the actual eye color as closely as I can.

Some other coloring options include mixing a bit of oil paint into the varnish when finishing to enhance an existing color. You could also stain, dye, apply food coloring, ebonize (add steel wool to vinegar to create a solution that darkens wood), and dilute paint. My preference is to leave the grain of the wood visible, which maintains a more natural look. Always test on scrap wood that is the same as the wood you plan to color for best results.

Wood Burning and Embellishments

Wood burning is another great way to spruce up a project. I have seen projects in which people have added facial details or other fine, delicate wood-burned lines. As with the rotary tool, there are many different attachments you can use with your wood burner, depending on the effect you want. It is best to practice on scrap wood before detailing your main project. Experiment with the different nibs to see what effects they produce.

Using a wood burner with various attachments is a great way to add small, intricate details to an intarsia piece.

Adding other elements into your work besides wood is a great way to add interesting effects to a project. Shells, rocks, gems—the options are limitless. For the carousel horse, adding reins made of real leather added the finishing touch needed to bring it to the next level.

There are many ways to make a project your own. I encourage you to explore the options and try some of these methods out.

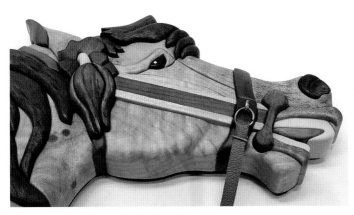

To achieve a more realistic effect, this project used leather instead of wood for parts of the halter.

Whales are majestic creatures that few people have the privilege of seeing. I'm very fortunate to live where I can catch glimpses of them during their annual migration. Some even live on the Oregon coast year-round. Several years ago, I went on a whale-watching boat tour in Alaska. It was the highlight of the trip!

This humpback whale fluke is a great project to get started with. It's easy to cut and you can focus your attention on the shaping. You can expect great results whether you just do the basic shaping or decide to get more creative.

TOOLS AND MATERIALS

- Wood: three shades of ¾" (1.9cm) blue pine, two types of ⅞"–1" (2.2–2.5cm) spalted maple
- Scissors
- Highlighter
- Pencil
- Utility knife
- Packaging tape
- Spray adhesive
- Square
- Drill press and small bit
- Oscillating spindle sander
- Flex drum sander
- Sanding pad and 220-grit sandpaper
- Gum eraser
- 220-grit sanding mop
- Waxed paper
- Wood glue
- Skewer
- Dowel (optional)
- Painter's tape
- Wood finish (I used a clear satin gel varnish)
- Paper towels
- Air compressor
- Disposable foam or glue brush
- Latex or nitrile gloves
- Rubber-tipped dental pick (or similar)
- Thin metal dental tool
- Sharp metal dental tool (or similar)
- Safety glasses
- Graphite tracing paper
- Awl
- L-clamps (however many needed to apply even pressure all over)
- Soft cloths or old socks
- Hanger kit

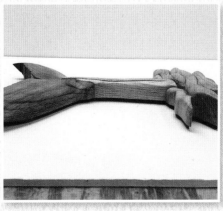

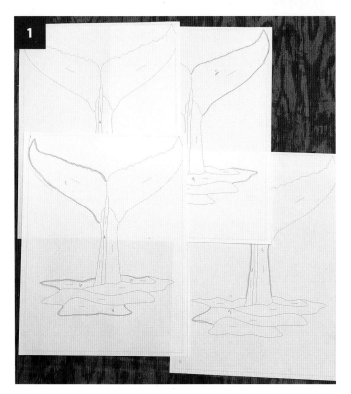

1 **Prepare the pattern.** Because of the way the pieces align, you will need four copies to cut pieces from, plus a master copy of the pattern. The photo above illustrates how each piece that will be cut out is numbered so that there are no other pieces around it that will also need to be cut. Begin by numbering the pieces on the master pattern. With the four copies, number one goes on the first page. If the next number touches the first, mark that piece on the second page. Continue numbering the pieces consecutively until all of them are on the pages and no two pieces to be cut adjoin each other on a single page. Next, use a light-colored highlighter to indicate the outer lines of the pieces marked if applicable. This lets you know you can relax a bit while cutting in the highlighted area since going off the line won't affect the fit. This is an optional step, but you'll find it beneficial.

2 **Select the wood.** I used blue pine and spalted maple for this project. Not only do they cut easily, but their wood grains also add a nice aesthetic touch. Check your boards on both sides before deciding on a piece of wood. I thought I'd found the perfect piece here until I turned it over. As you can see, the back has very little gray on it.

3 **Plan pattern arrangement.** Lay out the pattern pieces on the wood to find the best grain for each piece. Use the lines on the pattern pieces as a guide for the direction of the grain.

4 **Apply packaging tape.** Remove the pieces and apply clear packaging tape to the wood. This helps to lubricate the blade to make cutting easier. It also makes it easy to remove the pattern after the piece is cut out. Apply spray adhesive to the back of the pattern pieces and place them directly on the tape. Once all the pattern pieces have been applied, you're ready to begin cutting!

TIP

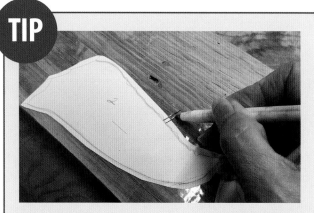

To ensure that you apply the pieces exactly where you want them, it helps to draw alignment lines through the pattern, continuing to the tape. Once you apply the spray adhesive, it makes it easy to place the pattern back where it goes.

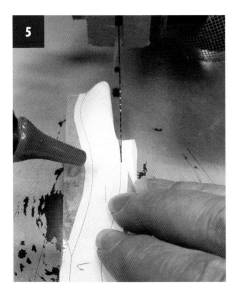

5 Cut out the pieces. Before you begin cutting, install a new blade. For this project, I used Platinum OnLine #7 reverse tooth blades. Because the wood I chose is softer, a #5 blade would also work. Use a small square to check that your blade is square to the table and make any necessary adjustments. When cutting, be consistent. Try to cut down the middle of the line.

TIP Sometimes it's easier to cut if you begin at the highlighted areas and can get a feel for how the blade responds to the wood before having to worry too much about staying right on the line. It's also helpful to draw a few lines in scrap areas and practice on those first. Every type of wood can respond differently. If you're new to the type of blades or wood you're using, it always helps to take a little test drive before cutting the pieces out.

6 Remove the fuzzies and assemble pieces. Once all pieces are cut out, remove the fuzzies or any burrs left from cutting off the bottom edges of each piece with a sanding mop. Hold the piece firmly, and lightly touch the edges of the bottom to the sanding mop. It doesn't take much pressure. This step will help the pieces fit together better by removing any waste that could get in the way during assembly. If you don't have a sanding mop, sandpaper will work. Then, transfer the piece number that's on the pattern cutout to the bottom of the piece itself. This will help with reassembly and prevent accidentally sanding the wrong side of a piece. This is a good habit to get into for all projects. Remove the pattern and clear tape from the top and assemble the pieces on the master pattern.

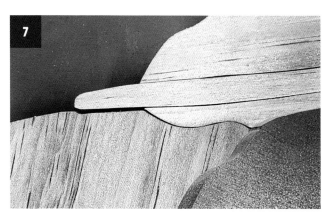

7 Check for minor fit issues. Carefully check the fit of all pieces. If there are any small gaps, you should be able to correct them by removing a small amount of material. Do this carefully, because it's easy to remove too much. If too much material is removed, or the fit is too far off, sometimes it's best just to recut a piece. In the photo above, the gap where the body meets the tail is causing the tailpieces to not align properly

8 Correct any fit issues. Using the smallest spindle on the oscillating spindle sander, gently remove a tiny bit of material wherever you find problem areas. Check the fit often and don't get carried away. Keep in mind that altering one area can affect other areas, particularly on larger projects. The domino effect of this can potentially ruin a project. To correct the gap in the tailpiece, I gently removed small amounts at a time, rechecking the fit often, until this gap was minimized significantly.

9 Mark the wood for contouring. Beginning with the tail, mark the area where you want to indent the wood to create a contour, so the body flows into the tail.

10 Rough shape the tailpieces. Using the 120- or 180-grit flex drum sander, sand where you drew your marks to create a dip. You need to hold the piece firmly and at an angle to achieve this. You want it lower on the bottom, contouring up to blend into the rest of the tailpiece. Repeat this step for the left tailpiece.

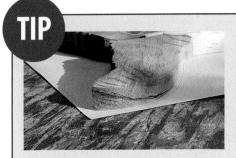

TIP

To add more dimension, you can back sand the ends of the tailpieces. First, draw a rough line on the side of the tailpiece as a guide for shaping. You want to leave a portion of the tail flat on the bottom so the backer has something to be glued to, but you can back sand as much or as little as desired. I went in about 1½" (3.8cm) and gently tapered up to the point of the tail.

11 Rough shape the body. Start by drawing pencil lines along the edges of the body pieces where they meet the tail and the water edges. Sand to the line drawn where the pieces meet the tail. Bevel the thin middle piece on each side slightly, and then mark where the other two sides meet it. Taper and soften the edges on the sides of the body until it flows with the tail and has a sleek look to it. The middle piece should be slightly higher than the two sides. Be careful not to sand the lower sides all the way down where these pieces meet the water.

12 Rough shape the water and mark where it meets the tail. When you're shaping the water, the top pieces should appear farther away and behind the body of the whale. The bottom pieces should appear closest to the viewer. This illusion of perspective is what creates the depth in this project. To show this, the furthest away pieces (the top) are the thinnest and the closest pieces (the bottom) are the thickest. The thicker pieces should be higher than the whale body. Because water is in constant movement, you can get as creative as you like with the contouring of the water. Then, use a pencil to mark where the shaped body adjoins the water pieces. Shape the two top water pieces down to below the side of the whale body. Add small dips and contours for more movement. Be careful not to shape the right end of the right piece too much because it has to fit into the adjoining piece below it, as well. They should end up around ¼"–⅜" (6.4–9.5mm) thick.

13 Prepare final water pieces. Next, draw a line on the next adjoining piece of the water. You want to keep the bottom portion of this piece higher (or thicker) to transition to the next piece, but the top of the piece needs to align with the piece above. It also should be higher than the whale body. Continue to add some dips to create extra movement in the waves. Draw a pencil line along the final water piece and shape to adjoin the piece above it.

14 Check for fit. In this and other project photos, you can see how the water builds up from ⅜" (9.5mm) up to 1" (2.5cm) from top to bottom. Reassemble the project and check for any areas that may need extra shaping.

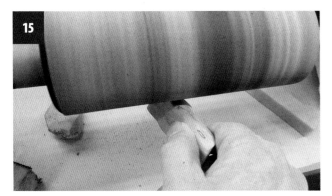

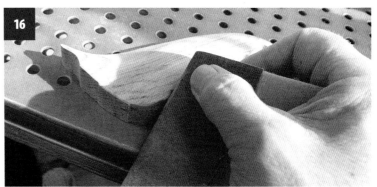

15 Sand the pieces smooth. Once you are satisfied with the general overall shape of the project, lightly sand all of the pieces with the flex drum sander using 220-grit. Be sure to sand with the grain. This will smooth out the pieces and remove any scratches.

16 Sand edges by hand. Using a thin foam sanding pad with 220-grit sandpaper, hand sand around the perimeter of each piece to soften any sharp edges. Align each piece with the surrounding pieces to check that each flows together with the next. You don't want any sharp edges that don't blend into adjoining pieces. Check for any scratches that you may have missed. Fine tune any areas that may need it. This is also the time to remove any pencil lines with a gum eraser.

TIP Once the sanding side of the thin foam pad wears out, I use regular sheets of 220-grit sandpaper cut into squares the same size as the foam pad. I simply hold the sandpaper and the foam together while hand sanding. This is much more economical. One foam pad will last many years this way.

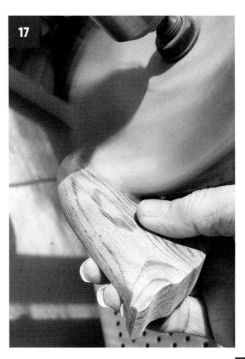

17 Buff the pieces. I like to give each piece a final buffing with a 220-grit sanding mop. This softens the edges, removes any fine scratches, and gives the pieces a nice, polished look. It's an optional step, but worth the results. If you used soft woods for this project, be gentle when using the sanding mop. If too much pressure is applied, you might add unwanted texture to the pieces. Some soft woods (such as pine) have varying densities of wood in the layers. If you apply too much pressure, it could cause a rippled, irregular surface. Be extra careful if using spalted wood for the water. It can be very soft in areas. Depending on how spalted it is, you may wish to skip this step altogether. Once you've finished buffing, place the master pattern on a smooth, flat surface and apply a sheet of waxed paper over it. Reassemble the project on the waxed paper.

18 Glue the body. When you're gluing any project, it's important to reassemble it often during the process to ensure that pieces don't get out of place. I use a skewer or sharpened ⅛" (3.2mm) dowel to apply dots of glue to the lower half of each piece. Start by gluing the body areas together.

19 Glue the tailpieces. Next, apply glue to the tailpieces, followed by the water pieces. Where the edges of the top water pieces meet the whale body, apply the glue sparingly to avoid squeeze out. If the pieces don't stay tight together on their own, use a piece of blue painter's tape as a clamp to hold them together until dry. This often happens with thinner pieces like the middle piece on the whale's body. Allow to dry thoroughly before applying finish.

20 Apply the finish. Because soft woods were used in this project, they absorb the finish more quickly than harder woods. To ensure even coverage, start at the top and work your way down. This will also help keep the coloring and absorption uniform. Start with the edges of the tailpieces. Don't forget the back sanded area. Continue to the front of the fins, the body, and finally, the water. If there are areas that dry too quickly, simply apply more finish.

TIP I prefer to use a clear satin gel varnish for the finish. It gives a smooth, professional, hand-rubbed look to the finished project. It doesn't require sanding between coats, which can be difficult if you glue your project together prior to finishing. It's very forgiving, especially if you finish your work in the same space that you cut and sand. Some types of finish, particularly sprays, can collect dust easily and once they dry, there is no easy way to eliminate the dust without additional work. This is my personal preference. Feel free to use what you prefer.

21 Remove excess finish. Using paper towels, wipe off as much excess finish as possible. With an air compressor, blow excess finish out of all the cracks and wipe the project off again. It helps to hold a paper towel over the air compressor while blowing. This will keep the finish contained to a small space. If you don't have an air compressor, a thin metal dental tool or something similar should get most of the excess finish out of the cracks.

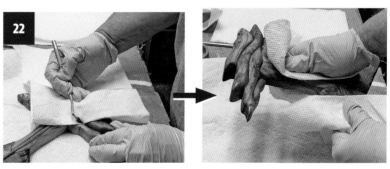

22 Remove excess finish from cracks. Use a rubber-tipped dental tool and clean paper towel to clean excess finish. Go around the edges of each piece, carefully getting into all the nooks and crannies to remove any residual finish. Check the edges of the project for excess finish as well. Sometimes the finish starts to dry before it's all removed and won't blow out of the cracks easily. Be sure to wipe the project down thoroughly, holding pieces to the light to find any areas you might've missed.

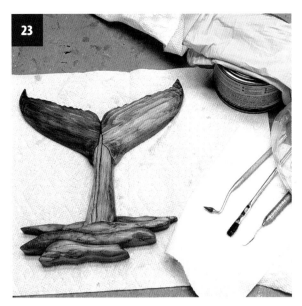

23 **Dry.** Allow the project to dry overnight and apply a second coat. You can apply an optional third coat if desired.

24 **Trace project onto the backer board.** The backing adds strength to a project and provides a professional finished appearance. For most of my projects, I use ⅛" (3.2mm)-thick Baltic birch plywood for the backing. If a project is very large, I will go up to ¼" (6.4mm) thick. Because there are areas where a pencil won't reach, I placed graphite tracing paper under the project and used a sharp awl to trace the outline onto the backer. This allows easy transfer of the outline to the wood. Use one hand to keep the project firmly in place so that the outline is accurate. Where the tail is back sanded, reach under with the awl to trace around where the flat part of the wood meets the backer. The backer won't be applied to the back sanded tips of the fins. They are meant to free float away from the wall once the project is hanging.

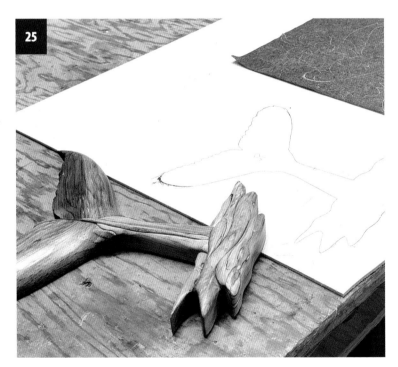

25 **Mark the backer and cut to size.** Mark "up" or "top" on the top of the backer so you sand the correct side and know on which side to apply the glue. If necessary, cut the backer piece to a manageable size so it is easy to cut out on the scroll saw.

26 **Cut out the backing.** Using a #3 blade or finer, cut out the backing. Cut approximately ⅛" (3.2mm) inside your traced line so that the backing isn't visible from the front of the finished piece. You may find it easier to control the cutting if the speed of the scroll saw is reduced. When cutting the curved areas, use the index finger on your dominant hand as a pivot point while you turn and guide it with your non-dominant hand. Use both hands to guide your piece through the saw blade while holding it flat.

27 Check the fit. When complete, test fit the backing piece to ensure no edges overhang the piece.

28 Sand the backer. With the sanding mop or sandpaper, soften the edges of the backer that will face out. Remove any fuzzies from the edges on both sides. Lightly sand the back of the backer piece by hand or with a sanding mop.

TIP

Be careful with any fragile areas that the sanding mop may catch, such as the narrow curves in the bottom of the piece. These areas can be sanded by hand if necessary. If the sanding mop grabs this area, the kickback can potentially cause the piece to stab you or fly off and break. If you do sand this area with the sanding mop, make sure the curvy areas point away from you so the sander is moving from the middle to the edge of the piece, not directly into this area.

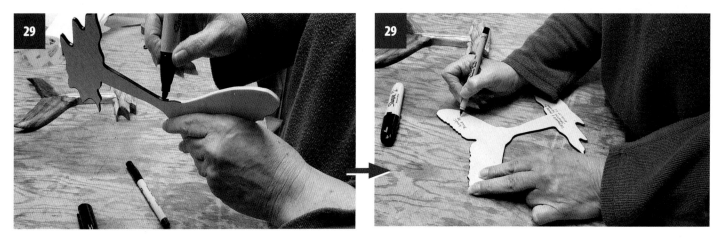

29 Color and sign the backer. To make the edge of the backer less visible once you hang the finished piece, color the edges with a wide-tipped permanent marker. If you keep the "up" side facing you, it's more difficult to accidentally slip and mark the visible side. I like to write the types of wood used on the back of each project. A fine-tipped marker or pen works well for this. Don't forget to sign your piece, as well. I also number my finished projects. It helps me keep track of them. If you sell your work, customers appreciate this.

30 Apply glue to the backer. Set the project upside down on something soft. Old socks work well for this. Apply glue to the "up" side of the backer and spread thinly and evenly, covering the entire area. Work quickly so the glue doesn't dry out. Don't leave any areas with excess glue or it could seep through onto the front.

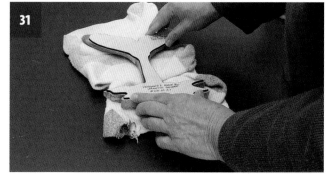

31 Adhere the backer to the project. Apply the backer to the back of the project and slide it around slightly so the glue makes good contact. Check all the edges carefully to ensure that the backer does not overhang the project anywhere and no areas of it are visible from the front.

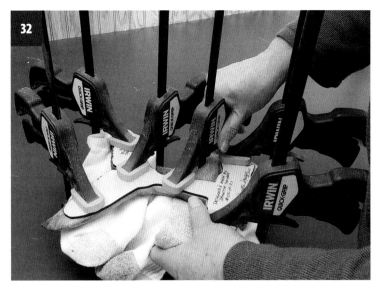

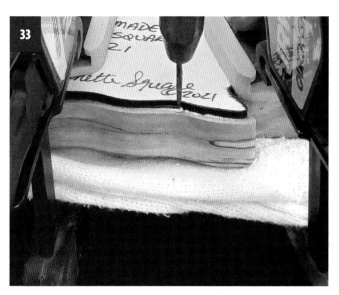

32 **Apply clamps.** Using the socks to protect the front, gently apply clamps all the way around and ensure every part of the backer is tight to the front. Make sure the backer hasn't slipped at all during the clamping process.

33 **Clean up glue and remove clamps.** Check around the edges for any glue that has seeped out. Use a skewer or an awl to remove any you may find. Allow to dry thoroughly, then remove the clamps.

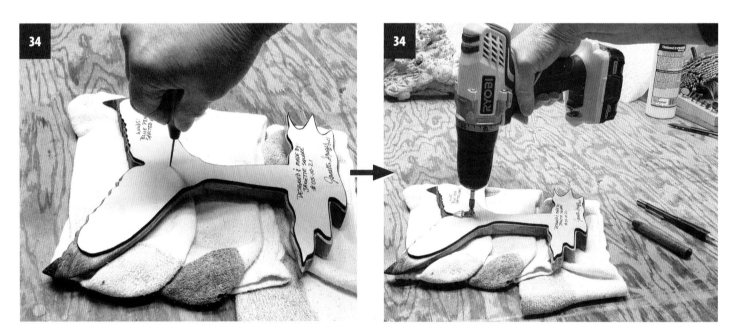

34 **Attach the hanger.** To attach a hanger, first find the balanced spot that allows the project to hang straight. It won't always be in the middle of your project. Use your thumb and forefinger to find the right balancing point. The whale body should be vertical. Mark this spot with a pencil. Poke a small starter hole with a sharp awl. Depending on the type of hanger you use, you may need to drill a small hole. If so, be very careful not to drill all the way through to the front. Finally, attach the hanger and proudly display your project.

TIP

If you find that your project doesn't hang quite straight, you can apply self-adhesive rubber bumper pads to the lower portion of the back of the piece. The bumpers will grip the wall, keeping your project exactly the way you want it to hang.

Succulent

Beginner

Pattern on page 116

Succulents are interesting and easy-to-grow plants. There are so many varieties, both for indoors and outdoors. I have amassed quite a collection of them on my enclosed porch. They never cease to amaze me with their interesting growth habits and hardiness, regardless of how much you ignore them. We occasionally have "fairies" that come by and leave little presents on the porch for me to discover, like this Aeonium kiwi—a beautiful little succulent that stays compact and tidy, is more tolerant of water than many succulents, and is easily propagated.

This is a great project for showcasing dimension, as all the leaves start as ¾" (1.9cm) thick, but their final thicknesses vary dramatically. These plump succulent leaves are the first of several projects that will show you different options for shaping leaves and flower petals. There's so much more to it than simply rounding over the edges. Getting creative with the shaping process is the key to becoming a great intarsia artist.

TOOLS AND MATERIALS

These dimensions are guidelines only. The size you use will depend on how you lay out the pattern pieces on the wood.

- ¾" x 8" x 12" (1.9 x 20.3 x 30.5cm) green poplar for the leaves. (I used scraps of darker poplar for two of the pieces for shading purposes)
- ¼" x 6" x 2½" (6.4 x 152.4 x 63.5mm) camphor burl for the pot. (Any wood with an interesting grain will do.)
- ⁷⁄₁₆"–½" x 3" x 1½" camphor burl for the rim of the pot. (Again, any wood with interesting grain works.)

- ⅛" x 8" x 8" (3.2 x 203.2 x 203.2mm) Baltic birch plywood (or wood of choice) for backer
- ⅛" x 3" x 3" (3.2 x 76.2 x 76.2mm) scrap piece of plywood for riser
- ¼" x 3" x 3" (6.4 x 76.2 x 76.2mm) scrap piece of plywood for riser
- Scroll saw blades, #3, #5, and #7
- Scroll saw
- Belt sander
- Sanding mop

- Sandpaper, 220 grit
- Sanding sponge or sanding block
- Spindle sander
- Flex drum sander
- Rotary tool and assorted burrs (check instructions for specific types)
- Wood glue
- Skewer
- Utility knife
- CA glue
- Utility knife
- Air compressor
- Sharp dental tool
- Rubber-tipped dental tool
- Awl

- Carbon or graphite paper
- L-clamps (however many needed to apply even pressure all over)
- Soft cloths or old socks
- Hanger kit
- Drill or drill press and assorted bits (check instructions for specific sizes)
- Clear packaging tape
- Spray adhesive
- Double-sided tape
- Highlighter
- Scissors
- Pen/pencil
- Waxed paper

- Wood finish (I use a clear gel varnish)
- Disposable foam or glue brush
- Latex or nitrile gloves
- Paper towels
- Black permanent marker
- Rubber bumpers (optional)
- Awl

TIP

Sourcing Wood

All of the wood used in this project is recycled. If you get creative, you can find many sources for wood that might otherwise go to the landfill or get burned. Several of my fellow woodworkers use cabinet shops as a source. They will often give away or sell the scrap pieces. I have a large box of "corners" of beautiful hardwoods from a fellow woodworker who made round rotating trays. Lumber yards often have bins of free scraps. These are all perfect for intarsia! We don't need large, perfect boards. Pallets can sometimes be made of exotic hardwoods, depending on their country of origin. What is domestic and abundant in another country can be like gold to us. Collecting wood for intarsia doesn't need to be an expensive endeavor and, in fact, can become a hobby in itself!

1 Highlight the pieces. Highlight the perimeter pieces that will be cut out. This will let you know while cutting that there are no adjoining pieces. I find this handy so I can relax a bit while cutting without worrying about staying perfectly on the line.

TIP Always begin cutting with a new blade. To prevent the blade from slipping once installed, clean each end by gently rubbing with 220 or higher fine-grit sandpaper. This removes any lubricant that was applied during the manufacturing process. It will also keep the blade clamps cleaner and free of residue buildup. Simply rub the top and bottom inch or so of the blade between the folded piece of sandpaper a few times, wipe off any residue, then install the blade into your saw.

2 Cut the pattern pieces. Cut out all the pattern pieces and apply clear packaging tape to the wood. For the smaller pattern pieces in the middle, cut out pieces **10** and **11** together, as well as pieces **12** and **13**. Lay out the leaf pieces on the wood using the lines indicated on the pattern as a guide for the grain direction.

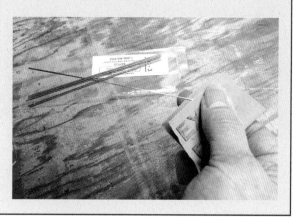

3 Adhere the pattern pieces. Apply spray adhesive to the back of the pattern pieces, a few at a time, and adhere them to the board. If needed, cut the board into smaller, more maneuverable segments.

4 Cut out the pieces. Cut one side of the smaller pieces first. Before separating them from the board, cut them apart from each other with a #3 blade. Switch back to a #7 blade and finish cutting the pieces. By using a finer blade to separate them, the kerf (space left by the blade) is minimized.

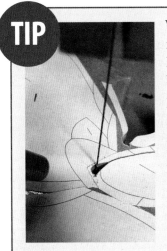

TIP

When you approach a sharp turn or the start of a new line, don't simply turn the wood quickly and hope for a square, sharp corner. If you do this, the blade can flex, which will cause the edge of the piece to flare out and create a poor fit. Instead, go past the line, back up and cut out a little half-moon-shaped hole. Then, you can start the next line, creating a crisp, square edge. The hole gives the blade space to turn, and the pieces will fit together much better.

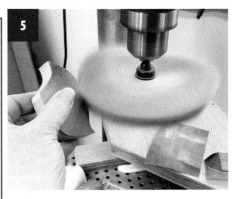

5 **Remove the fuzzies.** Once all the pieces have been cut, remove any fuzzies on the bottom. This can be done by hand or with a sanding mop.

6 **Number and assemble the pieces.** Number the bottom of each piece, then remove the pattern from the top and assemble the pieces on the master copy.

7 **Create a riser.** Cut out one ¼" (6.4mm) riser to be used for pieces **9 through 18** (all the center pieces).

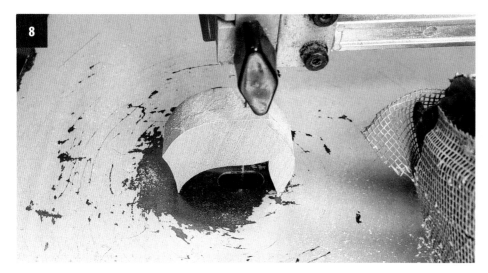

8 **Reduce the height of piece 2.** Turn the piece over and use a scrap of ¼" (6.4mm) plywood as the height gauge. Hold the pencil on the scrap wood against the piece. Move the piece along the edge of the pencil, drawing a line as you go. Then, cut along the line with your scroll saw. Hold the piece with both hands as you cut. Move slowly, letting the blade do the work.

9 **Create another riser.** Cut out a ⅛" (3.2mm) riser for **piece 7**. Because it's only one piece, simply trace the piece onto the riser material. Cut out the riser, staying inside the line by about ⅛" (3.2mm). The photo above shows all the risers in place.

10 **Rough shape the leaves.** Starting with **leaf piece 2**, begin rough shaping the leaves. For this, use the flex drum sander with 120- or 180-grit drums (this will apply to all rough shaping for this project). Taper the piece downward slightly toward the bottom. Scoop out the middle and round the outside edges slightly.

11 **Lower the pieces so they fit correctly.** Lower the sides of pieces **4, 6**, and **8** where they adjoin other leaves. For this, use your flex drum sander to gently taper the sides so they sit about ¼" (6.4mm) below the adjoining leaf pieces. For **pieces 6** and **8**, only lower where they meet with other leaf pieces, not where they meet the pot. The leaves should remain well above the pot. Lower **piece 1** where it meets **3**. It should sit below **3**, but above **2** and **8**.

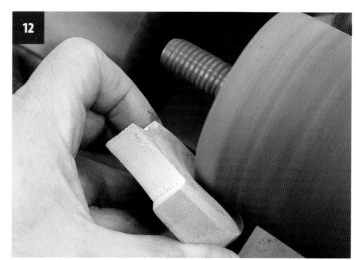

12 **Create a concave.** Mark the middle of each piece and scoop out the center of each slightly to give a bit of a concave appearance. This can be done with an oscillating spindle sander, a rotary tool, or the edge of a flex drum sander.

13 **Mark and rough shape the center pieces.** Mark the edge of the center pieces where they join the surrounding petals. This will keep you from sanding them too low. Round **piece 16** down toward **15** and add a dip in the center. This leaf faces the viewer at a different angle from the rest. **Pieces 17** and **18** are the underside of **piece 16**. Round these over on the bottom. The tops should align with **piece 16**.

14 **Rough shape the remaining pieces.** Taper **pieces 12** and **13** down toward **9**, and round the tops of each piece. **Piece 14** tapers down toward the middle and should sit lower than **13**. Angle the bottom of **piece 11** down to sit below the others. Curve its middle slightly. Its top should sit higher than all other pieces. **Piece 10** is angled down and to the right so the right side **is below 11**. It should also appear to be below **9**. Round over the left side of **9** and the right side of **15**. The edge of **15** sits below **9**.

15 **Sand the pieces smooth.** Once you are satisfied with the overall shape of the pieces, smooth them all out with the 220-grit flex drum sander, removing any scratches. Then, hand sand each piece with 220-grit sandpaper and a sanding sponge to soften the edges, being sure to go with the grain of the wood. Remove any pencil marks as you work your way through each piece.

16 **Buff and reassemble.** Buff each piece with the sanding mop. This adds a nice sheen and smooth look to the finished piece. Then, reassemble the project.

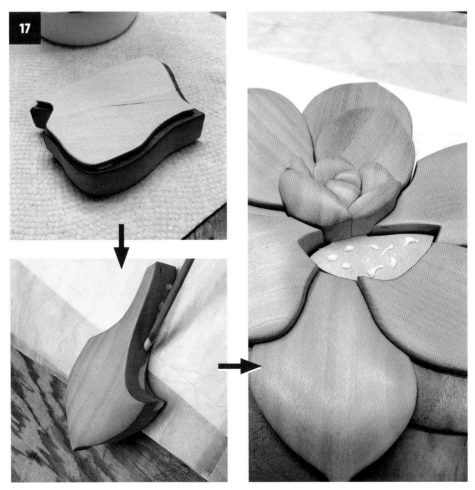

17 **Glue the pieces in their appropriate spots.** Glue the ⅛" (3.2mm) riser to piece 17. Then, edge glue all the pieces together (except the center pieces) with a skewer. Recheck the overall fit often to ensure the pieces don't shift. With the ¼" (6.4mm) riser in place, dot glue over the surface. Edge glue each center piece in place and to the riser. Allow the glue to dry thoroughly before applying finish.

18 **Apply your finish of choice.** I prefer to use a satin gel varnish. Wipe off as much excess as possible with paper towels. Then, use an air compressor to blow excess finish from the cracks and tight areas. Be sure to use eye protection, as the varnish can splatter everywhere. Using a rubber-tipped dental tool (or similar) and a paper towel, work around the edges of each piece to remove any remaining finish. If there is any remaining finish that has dried in the cracks, a metal pointed dental tool (or similar) works great for digging out these tight areas. Allow the project to dry overnight or according to packaging directions. Then, apply a second coat in the same manner.

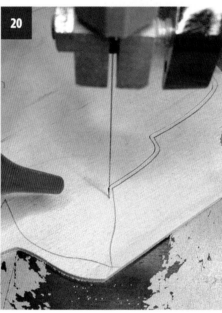

19 **Trace the project.** Using a pencil, trace the project onto the backer board

20 **Cut the backer.** Using a #3 or finer blade, cut out the backer. Stay approximately ⅛" (3.2mm) inside your line. To make coloring the edge easier, avoid cutting any inside sharp points. Instead, curve around the pointed areas, smoothly transitioning into the next petal.

21 **Sand the backing board.** Lightly sand the edges and back with the sanding mop or by hand.

22 **Color the edges and sign the back.** With a wide-tip black permanent marker, color the edges of the backer. This makes it less visible when the finished piece is hanging on the wall. Then, sign your name and, if desired, list the types of wood on the back.

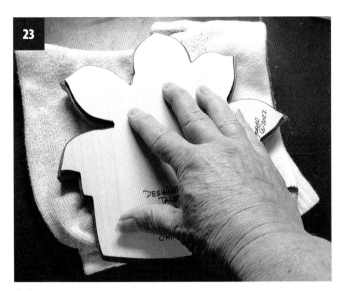

23 **Apply glue and adhere the backer to the project.** Apply glue to the "up" side of the backer with a brush. Place onto the back of the project and wiggle around to allow the glue to make good contact with the back of the piece.

24 **Clamp the project and remove excess glue.** Protect the front side of the piece with a soft cloth (I use old socks) and clamp the perimeter. If there is any glue seeping out the edges, allow it to set for a few minutes, then use an awl to remove any excess.

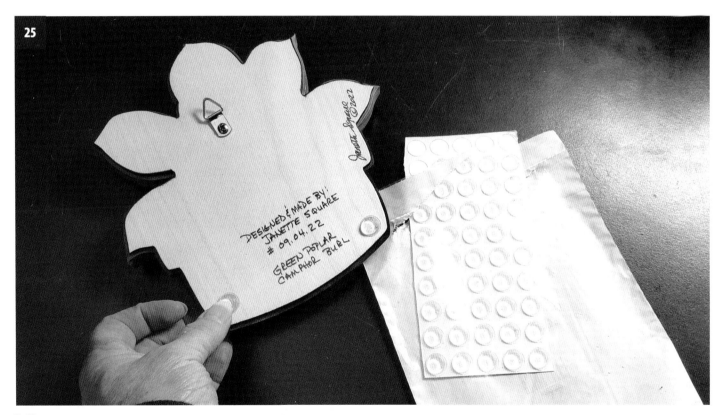

25 **Attach the hanger.** To apply a hanger, hold the project between your thumb and forefinger until it is balanced with the bottom edge of the pot horizontal. Make a mark where your thumb is. Make sure the mark is far enough down so that the hanger won't be visible. Use the awl to indent the spot marked. Place the hanger over the indent and attach with a screw. Be sure this is in a thicker area of the project so the screw doesn't pierce through to the front. Finally, hang and enjoy your hard work!

TIP

Always make a habit of checking the thickness where you want to drill. I like to apply clear bumpers to the bottom of the back. This helps the bottom sit further away from the wall and keeps it level once it is hanging.

Fish Magnets

Beginner

Pattern on page 117

About ten years ago, I created a tropical fish scene that was featured in *Scroll Saw Woodworking & Crafts Magazine* in the summer 2013 issue (#51). It proved to be a very popular design. This magnet is based on the cute little fish from that pattern. It can be used at its current size for magnets and ornaments, or as a simple wall art piece. It can easily be scaled up in size to create a focal point for any wall. You could also make an entire school of fish using a variety of wood colors.

This project will build upon skills discussed in the previous projects of this book. As such, I will not go into great detail for each step. For refreshers, consult Basic Steps of Intarsia on page 13. This is a great project for using up smaller pieces of scrap wood. It's also a good introduction to adding inlays within a piece. There are several projects throughout this book that include inlay pieces, and you will become a pro by the time you complete all of them! Different shaping techniques are demonstrated for each of the three fish created. This illustrates how you can vary one design to create multiple unique styles to make it your own.

TOOLS AND MATERIALS

Note: Listed here are the woods I used. I encourage you to get creative and use what you have on hand or can get easily. The thickness of the wood isn't critical, but you do want the pectoral fin to be thicker than the body so it will stand out. These wood sizes are only approximate. The size you need can vary greatly depending on how you orient the pattern pieces on the wood. I always recommend having larger pieces to give you greater options.

Fish One
- 7/8" x 4" x 3" (2.2 x 10.2 x 7.6cm) lacewood (body)
- 7/8" x 2" x 2" (2.2 x 5.1 x 5.1cm) sycamore (head)
- 3/4" x 3½" x 8" (1.9 x 8.9 x 20.3cm) butternut (dorsal, pelvic, and ventral fins; tail)
- 1" x 2" x 2" (2.5 x 5.1 x 5.1cm) aromatic red cedar (pectoral fin)
- 7/8" (2.2cm) aspen (scrap piece for spot on body)
- 7/8" x 2" x 2" (2.2 x 5.1 x 5.1cm) walnut (belly, head, and small piece on pectoral fin)
- 1/8" x 6½" x 4½" (3.2 x 165.1 x 114.3mm) Baltic birch plywood backer

- 5/16" x 1" (7.9 x 25.4mm) dowel
- 1/4" (6.4mm) rare earth magnet (or any strong magnet)

Fish Two
- 1" x 4" x 3" (2.5 x 10.2 x 7.6cm) maple burl (body)
- 7/8"–1" x 2" x 2" (2.2–2.5 x 5.1 x 5.1cm) spalted red alder (head)
- 1" x 3½" x 8" (2.5 x 8.9 x 20.3cm) aromatic red cedar (dorsal, pelvic, and ventral fins)
- 1" x 2" x 2" (2.5 x 5.1 x 5.1cm) aromatic red cedar (pectoral fin)
- 1" x 2" x 2" (2.5 x 5.1 x 5.1cm) butternut (for second pectoral fin, if needed)

- 1" x 2½" x 3" (2.5 x 6.4 x 7.6cm) spalted red alder (tail and belly)
- 1" (2.5) Peruvian walnut (scrap piece for spot on body, top of head, and small pectoral fin)
- 1/16" x 13" x 4½" (1.6 x 330.2 x 114.3mm) walnut veneer backer for two fish.
- 5/16" x 2" (7.9 x 50.8mm) dowel
- Two 1/4" (6.4mm) rare earth magnets (or any strong magnets)
- Acrylic antique white paint (highlight for eyes)
- CA glue (to apply magnets)
- Skewer (to apply dot to eye)

- 1/8" (3.2mm) or smaller drill bit
- 5/16" (7.9mm) brad point drill bit (for eye holes; adjust for dowel size you use)
- 1/4" forsner bit (or regular drill bit) to drill indents that hold the magnets (These may vary depending on the size of the magnets and dowels used.)
- Small ruler
- Rotary tool and assorted burrs
- Drill press or handheld drill
- Clear packaging tape
- Scroll saw
- Reverse tooth scroll saw blades— #7, #3
- Sanding mop (with 220-grit sandpaper)

- Pencil
- Highlighter
- Wood glue
- Spray adhesive
- Waxed paper
- Skewer
- Flex drum sander (with 220-grit sandpaper)
- Wood finish
- Paper towels
- Disposable foam or glue brush
- Latex or nitrile gloves
- Rubber-tipped dental tool (or similar)
- Sharp dental tool
- Air compressor
- L-clamps (3 minimum)
- Soft cloth (such as old socks)
- Awl
- Picture hanger and screw
- Drill

TIP Fish are popular subjects, and these are great to sell at arts & crafts shows or to give as gifts. Because magnets and ornaments tend to have a certain price point, I often would cut out the pieces for one fish, then slice the pieces in half to create two mirror images. I'll show you how that's done.

1 **Prepare and apply the pattern pieces.** First, decide if you're going to make one or two fish from one cutting. If you plan to make two, cut out an extra copy of the pectoral fin pattern piece. Then, prepare the pattern pieces and select your wood. Apply clear packaging tape onto the wood and attach the pattern pieces to the packaging tape with spray adhesive.

TIP **Choosing Wood**

Try to choose wood with an interesting grain or color. Now is a great time to dig through your supply of small pieces. The sizes listed for this project aren't critical and may vary depending on the orientation of the pattern.

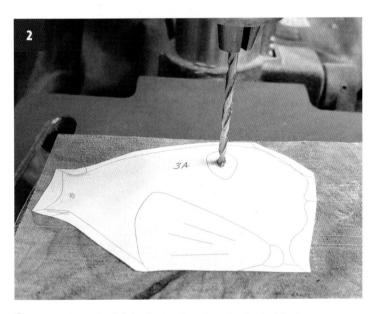

2 **Drill a hole in the fish body.** I prefer using a brad point bit whenever possible, as they produce much sharper holes. The smallest size I've found is 1/8" (3.2mm). The bit size isn't critical for the body piece; it just needs to be large enough for the blade to fit through and small enough to stay within the lines of the spot you will be cutting.

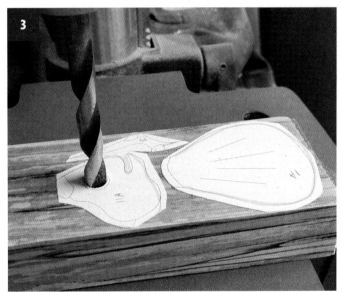

3 **Drill a hole for the fish eye.** For the eye, use a drill bit the same size as the dowel you're using. Set the height of the bit on the drill press so the point stops just below the table surface. Align the piece and drill the eye hole from the top. Only the point of the bit will come through the bottom. Turn the piece over and align the point of the bit with the hole from the other side and complete the cut. This method produces a clean cut with no tear out. Alternately, if using a handheld drill, put a piece of scrap wood under the piece when drilling. If you do get some tear out on the bottom, smooth it off before cutting the piece out.

TIP

It can't be stated enough: always begin a project with a new blade and check that it is square to the table. Getting into these habits is good practice. The cutting is straightforward for this project. It's important to take your time so the pieces remain square while cutting. The most likely reason that a piece is not square is from pushing it too hard while cutting. As the blade begins to dull, it's natural to start pushing harder without even realizing it. As soon as you notice yourself doing this, change the blade.

4 Cut all the pieces. These should be straightforward, but the hole in the fish body can be tricky. To cut it, unclamp the top of the blade. Feed the blade through the hole and retighten. Cut toward the line, turning clockwise until the blade is on the cut line. Cut a short distance on the line, then back the blade out. Spin your piece around and reinsert the back of the blade into the kerf you just cut. Continue the cut on the line in a counterclockwise direction. Slow down as you near the end to ensure the kerf aligns as you complete the cut. Cut a piece that fits into the hole in the same manner, using whatever wood you have selected for this.

5 Remove the fuzzies and check the fit. Once all the pieces are cut, remove any fuzzies from the bottom by gently using a sanding mop. This can also be done with plain sandpaper. Assemble the project on the master copy and check the fit.

6 Glue the small pieces. Glue the small pieces of wood you have selected for accents onto the head and the spot on the back. Allow to dry.

TIP

When you come across a tight curve while cutting, never force the blade around the corner. This will cause the blade to flex, and the piece won't fit correctly. Instead, nibble out a small opening at the turn before continuing. By doing this, you allow the blade room to turn without it having to twist or flex. Your curve will remain square and fit into the adjoining piece much better.

If you plan to make your fish into two fish, follow steps 7–9.

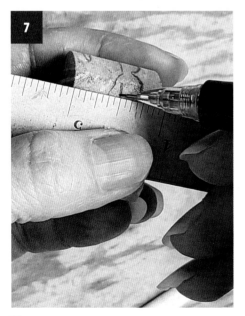

7 Mark the middle of each piece. Using a ruler to find the center, mark the middle of each piece except the pectoral fin. If desired, mark several spots and draw a line to make it easier to follow when cutting.

8 Cut along the lines you've made. Place each piece on its edge and cut straight down the middle. Keep the two halves of each piece together.

9 Assemble both the fish and its mirror image. In the photo above, the one facing right has the original bottom pieces. On the one facing left, the original top is now its bottom. Ensure that the original surfaces are now the bottom of each fish, or the pieces may not be square. Add the extra pectoral fin previously cut to the second fish.

10 Begin shaping. Shape the body and head first. The body is slightly rounded and tapered toward the tail fin. The head piece sits slightly lower than the body and is rounded. Rough shape the fins and tail to the general shape you're looking for before adding texture or contours. When using a rotary tool and burrs, it's always best to practice on a scrap piece of the same wood you want to carve. This gives you a feel for the burr and how it will work on the wood you're using.

For steps 11 and 12, I will provide multiple shaping options. Follow the instructions that are best suited to the look you'd like to achieve.

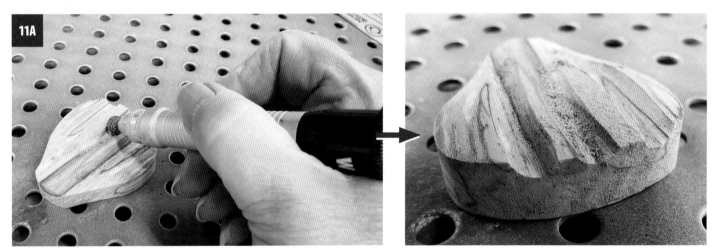

11A Create channels in the fish tail. A ball burr is great for gouging out dips to add a wavy look. Create three channels with the ball burr, then smooth and remove scratches with the flex drum sander.

11B Back sand the fish tail. Back sanding the tail fin can add to the three-dimensional look of the fish. Draw a rough line as a guide. Scoop out the middle of the tail fin so that it curves upward. Sand from the bottom up to meet the top edge. Always leave a portion of the bottom of the tailpiece unshaped where it joins the body so it will meet the backer and fully connect with the body piece. This will strengthen it.

12A **Create tapered indents.** Use a flame burr to create indents that are tapered on one end and wider on the other. Flame burrs are great for using on fins to add some motion. The narrow end is closest to the fish body and widens outward. Smooth the fins with the edge with the flex drum sander to remove scratches, then buff and soften with a sanding mop if desired.

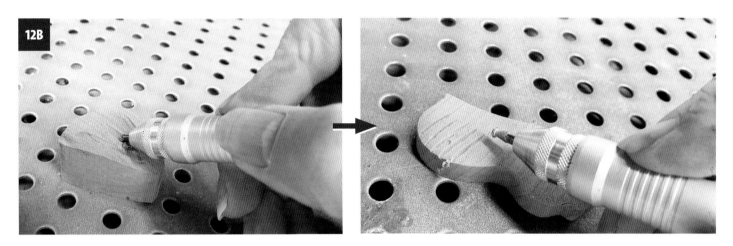

12B **Create narrow dips and lines.** A small ball burr is good for creating narrower dips. Draw a line to follow with the burr. Use a small knife-edge-style burr to create a series of lines for texturing.

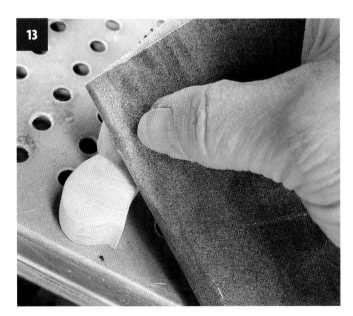

13 **Sand the pieces.** Hand sand each piece to soften the edges and fine tune the fit. Buff with a sanding mop.

14 **Round the dowel, soften, and check fit.** To make the fish's eyes, first round over the end of the dowel with the flex drum sander. Soften with sanding mop or by hand. Check the fit and, if necessary, sand the edges slightly until the dowel fits easily, but snugly, into the eye hole.

15 **Cut and color the eye pieces.** Cut the dowel by gently turning it while cutting so that the perimeter is cut, then finish cutting through it. This prevents any tear out on the edges. Color the surface and partway down the side of the dowel with paint or a black permanent marker.

16 **Glue the eyes in place.** The eye should protrude slightly above the head. I make the eyes shorter than the thickness of the head. This allows me to adjust the eye up or down as needed without having it push through the bottom. As long as it is a snug fit, it shouldn't sink into the head.

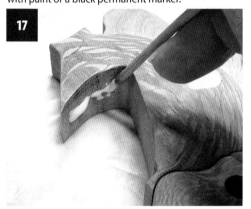

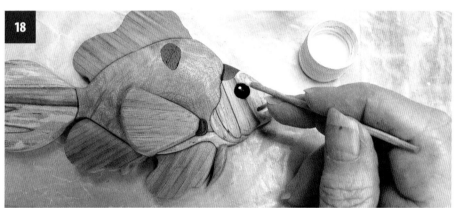

17 **Glue the project.** Glue the remaining pieces together and allow them to dry.

18 **Dot the eye.** With a skewer, apply a dot of antique white acrylic paint in the upper corner of the eye closest to the body. This brings the fish to life.

TIP
Backer Options

There are several options for the backer when you're making magnets and ornaments. If you're planning to make these fish into ornaments, I recommend adding a nice, thin backer, as it will be visible. I did this for the two thinner fish. I made the backer and glued it on prior to applying finish. This leaves a finished look on both sides. I used 1/16" (1.6mm) walnut veneer.

Another option is 1/8" (3.2mm) Baltic birch ply—my regular go-to backer. I did this for the single fish. In this case, apply the finish first, then glue the backer on as normal.

Yet a third option is to not apply a backer at all. Keep in mind that your project will be much more fragile without one. If you do omit the backer, gently sand the back of the piece with a belt sander prior to finishing. This will remove any dried glue, writing, or imperfections. Apply finish to both the front and back in this case.

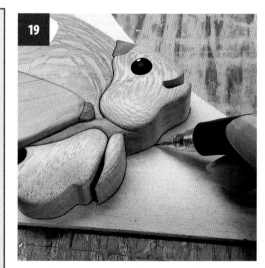

19 **Trace the project.** Trace the outline of the fish onto the backer (if you choose to use one). Where a pencil doesn't reach, an awl comes in handy to score the wood. Trace the score lines with a pencil before you cut.

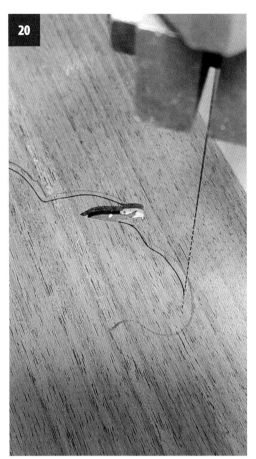

21 Apply the finish. By this point in the book, you should be getting the hang of finishing the pieces. Refer to the previous projects or the Apply Finish section on page 18 for more guidance.

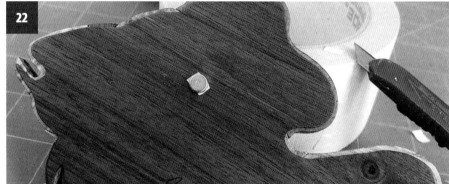

20 Cut out the backer. When cutting thin veneer, use a #2 or #²⁄₀ fine blade.

22 Test the magnet. Test the strength of the magnet by applying two-sided tape to it and the fish. If it is strong enough to hold up the fish, one magnet is sufficient. If the fish slides down or isn't secure, add a second magnet or use a larger one.

23 Mark where you will place the magnet. Hold the fish with your thumb and forefinger to find the center balancing point. Mark the spot on the back.

24 Inset the magnet. If you plan to inset the magnet, check the magnet size with a drill bit size gauge and use the same size drill bit to create an inset for the magnet to sit in. Then, cushion the finished side of the fish with a soft cloth while drilling the indent that will receive the magnet. Remove a little material at a time and check the depth frequently. Avoid drilling too deep. The magnet should sit slightly above the back of the fish. Check the fit, then glue into place. CA glue will hold the magnet securely (it might be necessary to place a bit of weight on top of the magnet to ensure adhesion). If you choose to turn your fish into an ornament, a small eye hook can be screwed into the dorsal fin for hanging. Use an awl to begin the hole, then gently screw in the hook. Fishing line or a thin ribbon can be tied to the hook for easy hanging.

Mermaid
Beginner

Mermaids are mythical creatures from the sea—or are they real? Who's to say they aren't? There's so much still undiscovered about life beneath our seas on this planet. We are discovering new species, previously unknown to us, all the time, and, real or not, this mermaid design is a great beginner project. It's not difficult to cut, and is an excellent one to hone your shaping skills. Her flowing hair creates wonderful dimension as it swirls around in the ocean's current. If you utilize several different shades of color, her hair is enhanced even more, showing off each color as it intertwines and flows.

The hair on the mermaid will hone your skills cutting accurate sharp points. I'll go over how to transition from one line to the next while cutting so that the edges stay crisp. Shaping the hair will help further develop your skills in adding dimension by creating varying thicknesses so that it appears to flow over and under adjoining hair pieces. The contouring of the tail fin in this project shows another option for shaping fins in general.

TOOLS AND MATERIALS

Note: Listed here are the woods I used. I encourage you to get creative and use what you have on hand or can get easily. These wood sizes are only approximate. The size you need can vary greatly depending on how you orient the pattern pieces on the wood. I always recommend having larger pieces to give you greater options.

- Figured maple (for lightest hair shade); ⅞"–1" x 6" x 7" (2.2–2.5 x 15.2 x 17.8cm)
- Butternut (for medium hair shade); ¾" x 6" x 12" (1.9 x 15.2 x 30.5cm)
- African mahogany (for darker red hues of hair); ⅞"–1" x 4" x 6" (2.2–2.5 x 10.2 x 15.2cm)
- Lacewood (for scales); ⅞"–1" x 4½" x 7" (2.2–2.5 x 11.4 x 17.9cm)
- Alder (for the body); ⅞"–1" x 2½" x 1" (2.2–2.5 x 6.4 x 2.5cm)
- Redwood (for the tail fins); ⅞"–1" x 4" x 12" (2.2–2.5 x 10.2 x 30.5cm)
- Scroll saw
- Scroll saw blades (check instructions for specific sizes)
- Belt sander
- Sanding mop
- Sandpaper, 220 grit
- Sanding sponge or sanding block
- Spindle sander
- Flex drum sander
- Rotary tool and assorted burrs (check instructions for specific types)
- Wood glue
- Skewer
- Utility knife
- CA glue
- Air compressor
- Sharp dental tool
- Rubber-tipped dental tool
- Awl
- Carbon or graphite paper
- L-clamps (however many needed to apply even pressure all over)
- Soft cloths or old socks
- Hanger kit
- Drill or drill press and assorted bits (check instructions for specific sizes)
- Clear packaging tape
- Spray adhesive
- Double-sided tape
- Highlighter
- Scissors
- Pen/pencil
- Waxed paper
- Wood finish (I use a clear gel varnish)
- Paper towels
- Disposable foam or glue brush
- Latex or nitrile gloves
- Black permanent marker
- Rubber bumpers (optional)

Pattern on pages 114 & 115

54   INTARSIA WOODWORKING MADE EASY

Preparation note: The pattern pieces have already been numbered for this project. It is easier to explain the shaping steps this way. You will need four copies of the pattern, plus a master copy. At this point in the book, you should be getting the hang of intarsia, so we won't get bogged down in too many details here. Refer to the Basic Steps of Intarsia section on page 13 for additional instruction.

1 **Cut out all the pattern pieces.** Select the types of wood you will use for this project. Try to find something with interesting grain for the mermaid's body. For the hair, I divided the pieces into three colors. Sort the hair pieces into the following piles: light-colored hair pieces (figured maple), piece numbers **2**, **4**, **7**, **12**, **14**, and **17**; medium-darkness hair pieces (butternut), piece numbers **1**, **5**, **6**, **8**, **13**, **15**, **18**, **20**, and **21**; darker-colored hair pieces, (African mahogany), piece numbers **3**, **9**, **11**, **16**, and **19**.

TIP

When selecting complementary wood colors, it helps to lay them out so you can see how they look together. To see what they would look like with finish applied, you can wet them slightly or apply mineral spirits to the wood's surface. Figured maple looks very light without finish but turns a lovely golden color once one is applied.

TIP

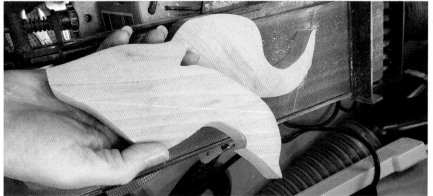

The redwood I used for the fins was rough on one side. When you come across wood like this, you can use the rough side facing up or down. The packaging tape adheres better to the smoother side and it's easier to see the grain of the wood. Be sure to sand the bottom flat before you begin cutting out the piece when using wood milled this way. A belt sander is handy for ensuring a perfectly flat surface. Never smooth the bottom of a piece after cutting it out. This could produce edges that aren't square, and the piece might not fit correctly.

2 **Adhere the pattern pieces.** Apply clear packaging tape to the wood and attach the pattern pieces to the tape with spray adhesive. I have a cardboard box open on two sides to use for spraying adhesive. This helps to contain the overspray.

3 **Begin cutting the pattern pieces.** For this project, there's no need to follow a particular order. Simply cut along the lines of your adhered pattern pieces. As always, remove any fuzzies and test the fit.

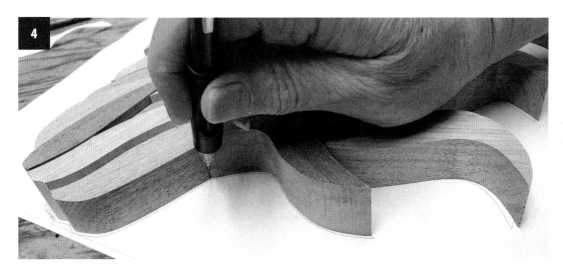

4 **Mark piece 1.** Beginning with **piece 1**, mark a small line where **piece 19** begins.

5 **Round over piece 1.** Round over the top and upper left side of piece 1 with a sweeping motion on the flex drum sander. Ensure you don't round over too far where **piece 19** will align with it. With all the hair pieces, always be careful when sanding the thinner ends, the wood will disappear more quickly than it does with wider pieces.

6 **Mark and shape piece 19.** Next, mark the edge of **piece 19** where it aligns with **piece 1**, then shape **piece 19**. It should appear to go under **piece 1** so you want it to be thinner, or lower, than **piece 1**. Lower the top, and taper toward the bottom slightly.

7 Continue shaping piece 19. Contour the bottom of the piece downward, then round over the entire left side. Keep the right side of the piece higher so it will end up above **piece 20**.

8 Shape piece 20. Shape **piece 20** the same way you shaped **piece 19**. The top should be lower than adjoining **pieces 1** and **19**. Curve the bottom and use the edge of the flex drum sander to get into the tighter, curved area. **Piece 21** is similar in height to piece 20. Where the pieces don't adjoin others, round them over completely so no edge line is visible. This creates a softer, more flowing look than leaving a hard edge.

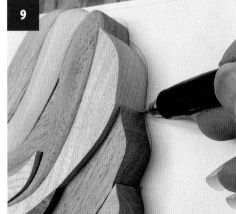

9 Mark the edges. For each piece, mark where the edge lines up to the previously shaped piece so you know where to shape to or go below. **Piece 18** should appear to be below its surrounding pieces and should align in height with **piece 20**. They form one continuous piece, with **piece 1** flowing over them. Always be aware of the pieces surrounding the piece you are shaping. Plan how each piece will relate to the pieces around it.

10 Continue shaping the hair. Using the progress and finished photos as reference, continue shaping the hair in this manner. The overall effect gives the appearance of pieces curving under and over each other to create a natural-looking flow, as if currents of the water are sweeping through them.

11 Mark where the hair pieces meet the body, then shape. Begin shaping by rounding over the sides. Body **pieces 10** and **22** need to flow together. To do this, utilize a sanding shim. Take a scrap piece of ¼" (6.4mm) plywood and attach the two pieces to it with double-sided tape. Shape them as if they were one piece. With the edge of the flex drum sander, create a slight dip in the lower back area. Taper the sides down all the way so there are no unshaped, sharp edges.

12 **Mark the edge of the tailpieces.** If the body piece is still higher than the tail where they meet, simply taper the end of the body more so that it's slightly below the tail fins.

13 **Shape the tail.** Begin shaping the tail by creating a dip in the outer side of the wide area closest to the body. Start higher where it meets the body, then dip down to the outer edges.

14 **Contour the fins.** Next, contour the inner area at the lower end of the fins so the appearance is that of a sweeping S. Gradually taper the bottom of the fins where they come to a point at the bottom.

15 **Check fit, and shape where needed.** Reassemble the entire project to check for any areas that may need additional shaping. Smooth sand every piece with the 220-grit flex drum sander to remove scratches and smooth the contours. Be extra careful with the sharp ends of the hair so you don't accidentally lower them too far while sanding. Every piece should feel smooth and end up evenly rounded.

16 **Sand the pieces and reassemble.** Hand sand each piece, reassembling the pieces as you go. Look at the edges as you go and see how they blend with the adjoining pieces.

17 **Sand the edges.** Hand sand the edges and sides so they are softly rounded and blend together smoothly. While sanding, check for any leftover marks or scratches and sand them out.

18 **Buff the pieces.** Soften the edges and buff each piece with 220-grit sanding mop. Once again, be careful of the sharp ends of each piece, as they can be easily damaged. I hold my finger on the sides of the area I want to protect. With very soft woods, such as the redwood used in the fin pieces, you may want to eliminate this step, as the pieces can break very easily, and you could also add unwanted texture.

19 **Glue the pieces.** Place the master pattern on a smooth, flat surface and lay waxed paper over it. You can tape it in place if you find it slides around too much. Beginning with the hair pieces, start with **piece 1** and work your way across. Dot the glue on the lower part of each piece as you go. Be careful of pieces that may slide out of position. To avoid this, reassemble the entire project periodically as you go. This way, you can ensure everything still fits as it should while the glue is still wet. Allow the glue to dry completely before applying the finish.

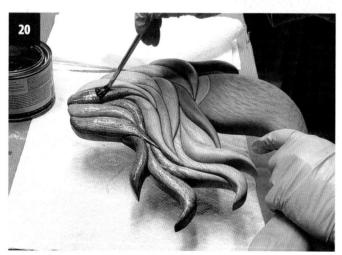

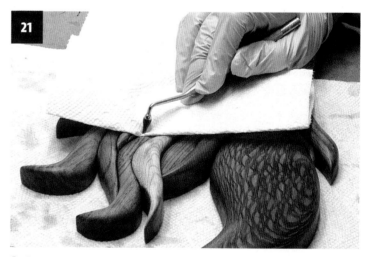

20 **Apply the finish.** I prefer to start at one end and work my way around so that the finish stays continually wet. This helps to prevent uneven absorption, which could show up as variations in the color.

21 **Wipe off excess finish.** Wipe off excess finish with paper towels in the same order it was applied. With a fresh paper towel, go over the entire project again and get into the crevices with your fingernail to get as much finish off as possible. As with our previous projects, you can use an air compressor to remove finish from crevices. For any remaining finish, you can use a paper towel and dental tools to get to the hard-to-reach places.

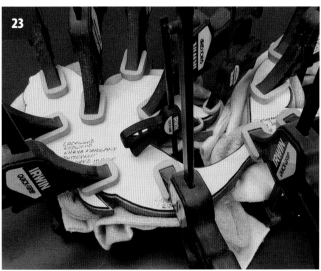

22 **Wipe down, allow to dry, and apply second coat.** Wipe the entire project down with clean towels and allow to dry thoroughly. Apply a second coat after the finish has completely dried.

23 **Prepare the backer and glue the project to it.** If any areas are hard-to-reach with a pencil, you can place graphite paper beneath the project and use an awl to score the hard-to-reach areas, then trace those with a pencil. Be careful with the sanding mop in the pointy areas. These areas are best sanded by hand for this project. Glue the backer on.

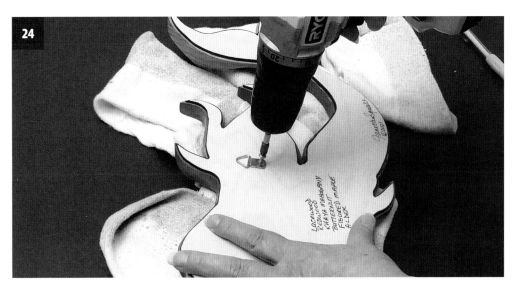

24 **Attach the hanger.** As usual, find your center point and mark it. Then, use a drill to attach your hanger.

Dogwood Flowers

Beginner

Pattern on pages 118 & 119

The flowering dogwood is a beautiful tree native to the eastern United States and parts of Canada. Its spring blooming flowers are a welcome sight after a long, dreary winter. As a bonus, they attract many beneficial insects to the garden. Because of its modest size and multiple seasons of interest, the dogwood's popularity has grown widely, making it an exceptional choice in landscapes around most the country. After the long-lasting flowers have gone, it produces beautiful fruit that birds love and provides a great show of vibrant and colorful red leaves in the fall.

This is a great design to learn how to shape flowers and leaves. Nature is seldom symmetrical or perfect, so shaping each petal is an opportunity to be creative and make it your own. In this project, the rotary tool is introduced. With it, you can get inventive shaping the petals and leaves. It's also used to add texture to the branches. Risers are incorporated to raise the center piece of each flower to add even more depth. The foundation for shaping flowers and how each petal sits above or below the ones beside it will give you a good sense of how dimensionality is created based on how you chose to shape your project. You will also learn how to create an open backer, drilling holes and cutting out all the openings within the project's backer to create an open, airy piece. This can be delicate work.

TOOLS AND MATERIALS

All these dimensions are approximate and subjective. The placement of the pattern piece can vary depending on the grain of the wood. You may, for example, put five pattern pieces in a long row and only utilize 2" (5.1cm) of width or put them across the piece, utilizing 10" (25.4cm) of width but only 3" (7.6cm) of length. I recommend having a larger board to give you options on pattern placement for any project you do.

- ⅝" x 5" x 8" (1.6 x 12.7 x 20.3cm) walnut for the branches
- ⅝" x 4" x 10" (1.6 x 10.2 x 25.4cm) green poplar (for the leaves)
- ¾"–1" x 4" x 7" (1.9–2.5 x 10.2 x 17.8cm) aspen (for the flower petals)
- ⅛" x 10" x 14" (3.2 x 254 x 355.6mm) Baltic birch plywood (for backer)

- Scrap pieces of spalted maple or other colorful wood for the center of the flowers
- Scroll saw
- Scroll saw blades (check instructions for specific sizes)
- Belt sander
- Sanding mop
- Sandpaper, 220 grit
- Sanding sponge or sanding block
- Spindle sander

- Flex drum sander
- Rotary tool and assorted burrs (check instructions for specific types)
- Wood glue
- Skewer
- CA glue
- Utility knife
- Air compressor
- Sharp dental tool
- Rubber-tipped dental tool
- Awl
- Carbon or graphite paper

- L-clamps (however many needed to apply even pressure all over)
- Soft cloths or old socks
- Hanger kit
- Drill or drill press and assorted bits (check instructions for specific sizes)
- Clear packaging tape
- Spray adhesive
- Double-sided tape
- Highlighter

- Scissors
- Pen/pencil
- Waxed paper
- Wood finish (I use a clear gel varnish)
- Paper towels
- Disposable foam or glue brush
- Latex or nitrile gloves
- Black permanent marker
- Rubber bumpers (optional)

1 **Prepare the pattern, select wood, and adhere pattern pieces.** For this project, you will need at least three copies of the pattern plus the master copy to set your pieces onto. Follow all usual preparation steps. If you need a refresher, see the Basic Steps of Intarsia section on page 13 or consult previous projects.

TIP

Selecting Wood

Dogwood flowers are primarily white or pink. Aspen is a good choice for this project, as it doesn't have much visible grain once shaped. It's also a softer wood and easier to shape. The branch can be any darker wood. I chose walnut because I had it on hand and it's easy to cut and shape. The green wood for the leaves is poplar. If you look through the boards at a lumber yard, you're bound to find some with green coloring in it. It's easy to cut and shape.

2 **Cut out the pieces.** Since this design has fewer adjoining areas, cutting should go quickly. I used a #7 reverse tooth blade for cutting. For the thinner branch and leaf pieces, you may wish to use a #5 blade for more control. Keep both halves of the leaf pieces together for now. It is easier to shape them first, then separate the segments. Once cut, remove the fuzzies from the back of all the pieces. This will create a better fit. Transfer the numbers to the back of the pieces and remove the pattern on all pieces except the leaves.

3 **Shape the petals of the left flower.** For the first step in shaping the pieces, I utilized a typhoon flame burr for rough shaping. You want the petals to curve slightly downward on the outside edges. Scoop out the middle to give a concave appearance. After shaping the first petal, mark the edge of the adjoining petal with the height.

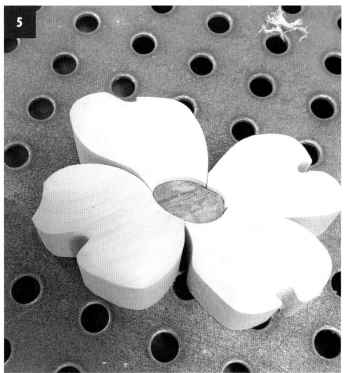

4 **Smooth the petals.** Once you are satisfied with the overall shape, smooth each petal with the edge of the flex drum sander. This will get into the center that is curved inward to eliminate all scratches.

5 **Check the fit.** Check the fit of the center piece. If necessary, add a riser to bring the height up so it sits at least ⅛" (3.2mm) higher than the petals. Create the riser by tracing the piece onto a scrap piece of ⅛" or ¼" (3.2 or 6.4mm) plywood. Cut out the riser just inside the line. Glue to the underside of the center piece to give it the necessary height. Don't forget to remark the "up" arrow on the underside to orient it correctly.

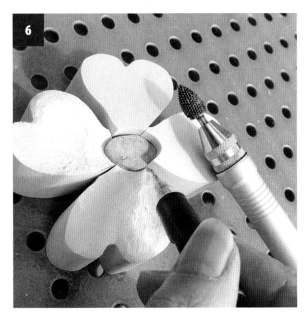

6 **Shape the petals of the right flower.** Mark where the two flowers meet so you can determine the height of that petal. Where the petals meet, you want the petal from the left flower to end up at least ¼" (6.4mm) higher than the right. Shape as you did for the first flower, marking where the adjoining petal sits. Be aware of where the branch and leaf pieces meet the petals so you don't sand the pieces too low. Overall, the flowers should sit significantly higher than the branches or leaves. Work your way through each petal, then sand with the flex drum sander as you did for the first flower.

7 **Check the height and fit.** Reassemble the two flowers and check the overall height of each petal.

Shaping Flowers and Leaves

With flowers, some petals sit above others, and some sit below. For these dogwood flowers, the differences are subtle but still apparent. On the left flower, the top petal sits slightly lower than the rest. For the right flower, the petal on the right is lowest. The top left petal should be lower than the petal beneath it. The middle of each petal where they join the center piece are all within 1/16" (1.6mm) or less of each other. Have fun with the shaping of the petals, there is no wrong way. Nature produces some interesting shapes of its own! When using the flex drum sander to shape, keep in mind that the amount of pressure you use will affect the shape that results. If you press harder, it will push the foam in and produce a rounder shape. A light touch will keep the piece flatter.

There are several ways to shape leaves. You can experiment with techniques to see what you prefer. I like to incorporate multiple sanding tools for the best variety.

A flame burr on the rotary tool is useful for creating the overall shape, adding the rough contour to the leaf piece.

The smallest ¼" (3.1cm) spindle on the oscillating spindle sander is ideal for creating an indent on the tapered end of the leaf. This gives the appearance of the leaf being slightly curved, adding additional interest.

The flex drum sander can also create curves and is the best tool for smoothing out scratches and rounding the pieces.

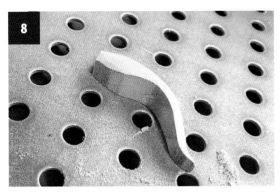

8 Begin shaping the leaves. Remove the pattern from the leaves, being sure that they are numbered on the bottom. Save the pattern pieces. Shape the smallest single leaf on the far right down to about 1/4" (6.4mm) and taper down toward the right.

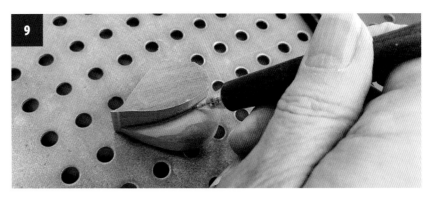

9 Shape the heart-shaped leaves. I shaped the two heart-shaped leaves a little differently. Rather than create the contour of the entire leaf piece, I cut them in half before contouring. The leaf is lower in the center and curves upward toward the sides. Cut the two heart-shaped leaves in half and remove the pattern. Shape the right half of the leaf so that it tapers inward (lower) towards the center. Mark the left half following the contour of the right. Shape the left half in the same manner so it also curves in toward the center and the outer edge is higher. Then, slightly round the top part of the leaf, being mindful of where the branch pieces adjoin.

10 Reattach the pattern and assemble the pieces. Once all of the leaves have been shaped, reattach the pattern pieces for the ones that need to be cut in half. Alternately, you can draw a line from point to point if you prefer. Separate these leaf pieces and reassemble into the project.

11 Shape the branches. I wanted to have the branch pieces textured to give the impression of bark. This is achieved by using the flame burr and rotary tool. Begin by drawing reference lines where the branch pieces meet other pieces. This gives you an idea of how low to shape. Shape each piece by removing material on the top as well as texturing the sides of each piece. Go with the grain so that the texture appears natural. Always be aware where adjoining pieces line up so you don't over shape that side. The branches should all sit lower than the leaf and flower pieces. Generally, the overall height of the branch pieces should be higher on the left side of the project and taper lower toward the right.

12 Smooth the bark pieces. Once you are satisfied with the shape of each piece, smooth off some of the roughness with a mop sander. By skipping the flex drum sander step, you are left with a textured look that resembles bark.

13 Shape the flower center and small leaves that surround the left flower. Shape the flower centers so they are rounded, but sit above the petals. Shape the small, lighter green leaves that adjoin the left flower. These should sit significantly lower than the petals so they appear to be behind them. The points should taper slightly downward. Reassemble the project and fine tune any areas that stand out.

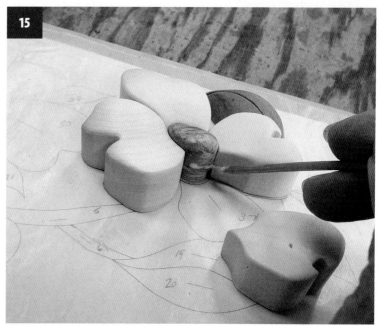

14 **Sand all the pieces.** Go over each flower and leaf piece with the 220-grit flex drum sander to smooth all areas. Hand sand the edges to soften and fine tune each piece. Remove any pencil marks you find along the way.

15 **Glue the leaves and flowers.** This project can be a bit tricky to glue together. Getting all the pieces to fit and stay where they belong is a bit challenging. The entire project is assembled and glued together after the finish has been applied. Use a piece of waxed paper over the pattern to prevent glue from getting on the pattern. Refer to the pattern to see where to apply the glue so you don't put it on areas that will be exposed. Starting with the center of the flower in place, apply glue to one petal at a time. Glue the two halves of each leaf piece together. You can glue several segments together where there are no fragile areas prior to finishing. Allow to dry thoroughly.

16 **Apply the finish.** Apply small amounts of blue painter's tape to the ends of the branches, leaves, and flowers where other pieces will be joined. This keeps the finish off the area and allows for better glue adhesion. Using a foam brush, apply the gel varnish. Don't apply the finish to all the pieces at once. Work in small groups of pieces, applying and removing excess finish before moving on to another group. First remove excess finish with a paper towel, then use a dental tool to go around each piece to remove any remaining varnish from the nooks and crannies. An air compressor is handy for getting excess finish out of the cracks as well. Allow to dry thoroughly and apply a second coat in the same way.

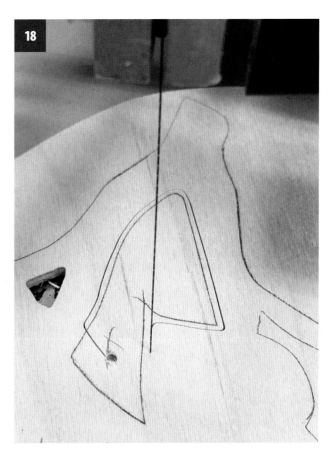

17 **Remove tape and glue the pieces together.** Remove all the blue painter's tape. Assemble the entire project on waxed paper covering the master pattern. Apply small amounts of glue, continuously reassembling the entire project until all pieces are glued together.

18 **Create the backer.** This is a delicate project. I chose to create a non-visible backer for it. Another option would be to find a nice solid piece of wood and simply glue the entire project to it. To create the regular backer, lay graphite or tracing paper over the plywood and place the project on top. Orient the project so the grain of the backer is in line with the length of the project. This will create the most strength. Use an awl to trace around the perimeter and all the internal openings of the project. You should end up with six openings that will need to be cut out. Mark the openings with an X and drill blade entry holes in each. Using a fine blade (#2 or #3), cut out the openings before cutting out the perimeter. This creates less chance of breakage of the delicate pieces. Cut the perimeter, then carefully hand sand any fuzzies around the edges. Label the back with your wood choices and sign it.

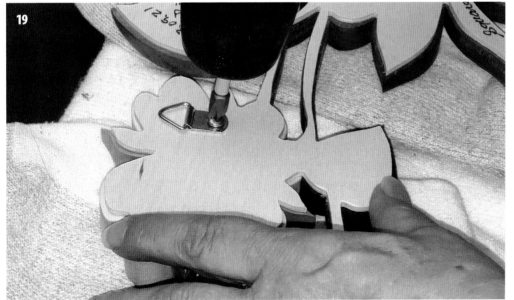

19 **Glue the project to the backer and attach the hanger.** Protect the surface and gently clamp or rest something heavy on top to allow good glue adhesion. Be careful not to apply too much glue to the thin areas. Any squeeze out can be removed with an awl. Allow to dry thoroughly. Find the balance point of the piece and apply your hanger. It should fall behind the left flower. Be careful that you don't apply it to an area where it could come through to the other side.

Ladybug on a Flower
Intermediate

Pattern on pages 120 & 121

Everyone loves ladybugs! Besides being cute, they serve an important purpose in the garden. They're voracious hunters when it comes to ridding your garden of aphids. Most people welcome them into their gardens—and this design is set in a garden, as well. I designed her sitting in a lovely yellow wildflower that grows in abundance locally. You can do a lot with the pattern: change the flower colors, experiment with different shaping techniques on the petals, or add texture to the flower's center. It makes a great gift for nature lovers and can easily be scaled up in size to create a dynamic focal point on someone's wall.

There are multiple spots to cut out for the ladybug, so you will hone your skills in cutting well-fit pieces to be glued in and shaped as part of a larger piece. This project also explores dimension by using thinner and thicker wood. Finally, we will cover additional ways to create texture, and ways to correct gaps that appear during glue-up.

TOOLS AND MATERIALS

Note: Listed here are the woods I used. I encourage you to get creative and use what you have on hand or can get easily.

- 5⁄8" x 4½" x 24" (1.6 x 11.4 x 61cm) yellowheart (for petals)
- 5⁄8" x 4" x 3" (1.6 x 10.2 x 7.6cm) figured redwood (for flower center)
- 1" x 4" x 3" (2.4 x 10.2 x 7.6cm) aromatic red cedar, Peruvian walnut, and aspen (for ladybug)
- 1⁄8" x 6½" x 4½" (3.2 x 165.1 x 114.3mm) Baltic

- birch plywood backer; it will be helpful to keep some scrap pieces for sanding shims and risers
- Scroll saw
- Scroll saw blades (check instructions for specific sizes)
- Belt sander
- Sanding mop
- Sandpaper, 220 grit
- Sanding sponge or sanding block
- Spindle sander

- Flex drum sander
- Rotary tool and assorted burrs (check instructions for specific types)
- Wood glue
- Skewer
- CA glue
- Utility knife
- Air compressor
- Sharp dental tool
- Rubber-tipped dental tool
- Awl
- Carbon or graphite paper

- L-clamps (however many needed to apply even pressure all over)
- Soft cloths or old socks
- Hanger kit
- Drill or drill press and assorted bits (check instructions for specific sizes)
- Clear packaging tape
- Spray adhesive
- Double-sided tape
- Highlighter

- Scissors
- Pen/pencil
- Waxed paper
- Wood finish (I use a clear gel varnish)
- Paper towels
- Disposable foam or glue brush
- Latex or nitrile gloves
- Black permanent marker
- Rubber bumpers (optional)

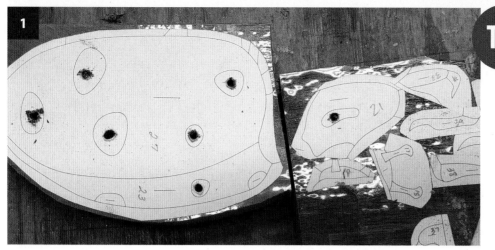

1 **Prepare the pattern and drill holes.** You will need five copies of the pattern, plus a master copy. The flower petals are numbered on the pattern to help keep them organized. Once all the pattern pieces have been attached, use a ⅛" (3.2mm) drill bit to drill holes in the ladybug body where the six black spots will be and in the head piece where the white inlay piece goes. Be sure the bottoms of the pieces are flat after drilling. Remove any tear out if needed.

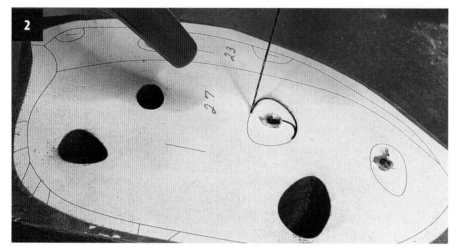

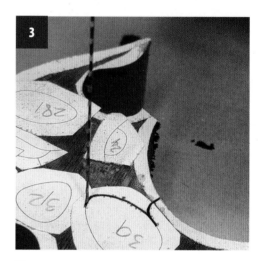

2 **Cut out the holes for the spots on the ladybug.** Insert the blade into the drilled hole. Cut toward the edge and turn clockwise (turning your piece counterclockwise). Cut a short distance in this direction. Back the blade out into the hole. Then, reverse the piece and feed the blade backward into the kerf you just made. Cut counterclockwise around the entire hole. Stay right on or just inside the line as you cut. Pop the waste piece out and remove the blade. This method helps to eliminate an uneven edge within the hole where you end the cut that can happen when you complete a full circle all in one direction.

3 **Complete the cuts.** Cut the spots that go into the holes the same way. Remember where on the line you followed when cutting the holes and cut the exact same way for the spots to ensure a tight fit.

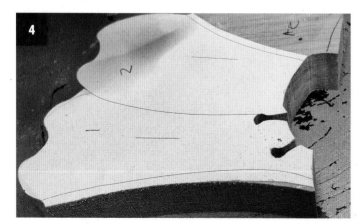

4 **Cut the petals.** Cut around the perimeter of **pieces 1** and **2**. Before separating, cut out the space for the ladybug antennae, then separate the pieces.

5 **Number your pieces.** Number each piece after cutting. For the very small pieces, write the number on the lower edge. This will let you know the piece number and help prevent sanding the wrong side. Then, assemble and check the fit.

6 **Glue the spots into the ladybug body.** Glue the white pieces to the black headpiece. Apply the glue from the bottom sparingly. This will prevent glue from getting onto the surface.

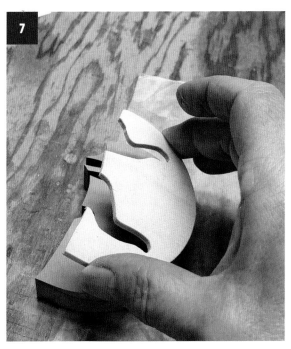

7 **Add riser (optional).** If necessary, add a riser to the flower center. My centerpiece was ⅝" (1.6cm). I added ⅛" (3.2mm) riser to bring the height up to ¾" (1.9cm).

8 **Mark the petals.** On a real flower, some of the petals are behind others, some have both sides on top, and others have both sides under the neighboring petals. To recreate this effect with intarsia, first mark the sides that sit under another petal with arrows to assist you in shaping them. You will be lowering those sides so they appear to be behind or underneath the adjoining petal.

9 **Shape piece 15.** With petal **piece 15**, lower the left side so it is below the edge of piece 14. Leave the right side at full height.

10 **Shape the remaining petals.** For **piece 1**, both sides will be lower than the adjoining petals. Reduce the thickness with a coarse-grit flex drum sander. Taper the sides to the desired height first, then use the edge of the sander to slightly scoop out the middle of the petal. If desired, add a dip at the end of the petal the same way. Do this for each petal as you're shaping it. Continue with petal **piece 2**, shaping the right side lower to fit under petal **piece 3**. **Pieces 5, 8,** and **12** have both sides of petals higher than those surrounding them. Pieces **1, 6,** and **9** have both sides lower than surrounding petals. Shape each petal in this manner until the circle is completed.

11 **Reassemble and check fit.** Reassemble all the pieces to check the overall look.

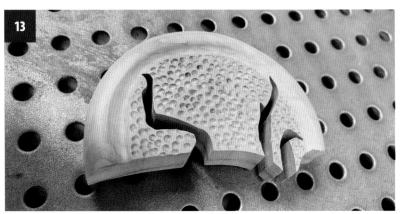

12 **Shape the flower's center.** Draw a light line around the centerpiece edge where the petals meet it. Shape the flower center by rounding over the edges. You may find it necessary to go back and adjust the ends of the petal pieces where they meet the center so that they remain lower than the flower's center.

13 **Add texture to the flower's center.** I used a small, ball-shaped burr to create tiny indents in the flower center as well as the rim. Practice your technique on a piece of scrap that is the same wood used for the flower. I went back over the piece several times, adding more indents and deepening others until the desired look was achieved. Power carving burrs work differently on different types of wood, so it is important to practice first on the type of wood you're using to get a feel for how easily or difficult it is to control and what the results will look like.

14 **Create a sanding shim.** Trace the ladybug body onto ⅛" (3.2mm) Baltic birch ply. Cut out a sanding shim for the ladybug body (one shim for both red pieces). If a riser will be needed for the ladybug, you can use the same piece for this later. Attach the two body pieces to the sanding shim with two-sided tape. Draw edge lines to indicate where adjoining pieces are.

15 **Taper the ladybug's body.** The ladybug should appear to be on angle with its right side farther from the viewer. Taper the top of the body down to just above where the petals meet. Round over the bottom part of the body slightly.

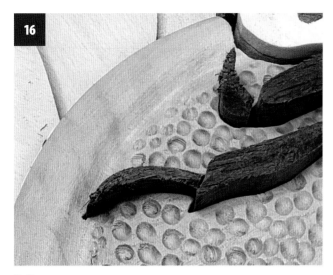

16 Shape the legs. Shape the legs so that each segment is slightly lower on the right side than the left.

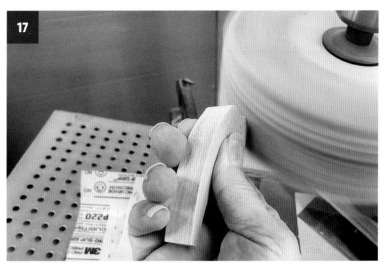

17 Sand all the pieces, then buff. Use the 220-grit flex drum sander to sand all the pieces. Then, hand sand to finish them off. After that, buff the project.

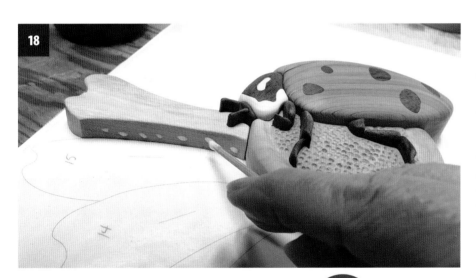

18 Glue the project and apply finish. Glue the ladybug body pieces together and to the riser, if applicable. Apply glue to the openings for the legs from the back of the piece, then insert the legs. Glue ladybug body and head together and to the center flower piece. Apply glue in dots to the lower area of the petal edges. Continue your way around until complete. Allow to dry thoroughly before applying finish. Once dry, apply your finish following the usual steps.

19 Cut the backer, adhere the project, and apply the hanger. Trace and cut out the backer. Adhere it to the project and attach the hanger following the usual methods. For more instruction, see the Basic Steps of Intarsia section on page 13.

TIP

Occasionally, an unintentional gap will magically appear after gluing. It happens to the best of us. One way to address this is to use a black marker on the glue side of the backer board where it will be visible through the mysterious gap. First, see where the gap falls on the backer, then color it in with the marker. The black will make the gap appear more as a shadow and be less visible. You can also use black matte spray paint and cover the entire surface if there are multiple gaps. Another option is to cut out the backer so that the gap appears intentional. After all, flowers are nature's creatures and it's entirely possible that there is "supposed" to be a gap there!

Buoys on a Fence Post

Intermediate

Pattern on pages 142–145

I am greatly inspired by my surroundings here in Yachats, on the Central Oregon Coast. Buoys and rope are abundant on fences as part of local yard art. Our split-rail fence is no exception, covered in a large assortment of buoys and ropes that we've rescued over the years.

This project will provide you with experience building your skills creating dimension by utilizing varying thicknesses of wood as well as the use of risers. Accurate cutting skills are further developed by creating the buoys with multiple colorful pieces which become one piece when shaped. Any gaps stand out more with this technique, so accurate cutting is important. You will also learn to make rope, which will require a bit of patience and a great attention to detail.

TOOLS AND MATERIALS

Note: Listed here are the woods I used. I encourage you to get creative and use what you have on hand or can get easily. These wood sizes are only approximate. The size you need can vary greatly depending on how you orient the pattern pieces on the wood. I always recommend having larger pieces to give you greater options.

- Round buoy, 1½" x 7" x 7" (3.8 x 17.9 x 17.9cm) redwood; 1½" x 2" x 7" (3.8 x 5.1 x 17.9cm) western red cedar
- Top left buoy, 1" x 4" x 3" (2.5 x 10.2 x 7.6cm) red cedar; 1" x 4" x 5" (2.5 x 10.2 x 12.7cm) aspen; 1" x 4" x 2" (2.5 x 10.2 x 5.1cm) Alaskan yellow cedar
- Top right buoy, ¾" x 5" x 2" (1.9 x 12.7 x 5.1cm) juniper; ¾" x 5" x 3" (1.9 x 12.7 x 7.6cm) aspen; ¾" x 5" x 1" (1.9 x 12.7 x 2.5cm) Alaskan yellow cedar; ¾" x 5" x 4" (1.9 x 12.7 x 10.2cm) green poplar

- Scroll saw
- Scroll saw blades (check instructions for specific sizes)
- Belt sander
- Sanding mop
- Sandpaper, 220 grit
- Sanding sponge or sanding block
- Spindle sander
- Flex drum sander
- Rotary tool and assorted burrs (check instructions for specific types)
- Wood glue
- Skewer
- CA glue
- Utility knife

- Air compressor
- Sharp dental tool
- Rubber-tipped dental tool
- Awl
- Carbon or graphite paper
- L-clamps (however many needed to apply even pressure all over)
- Soft cloths or old socks
- Hanger kit
- Drill or drill press and assorted bits (check instructions for specific sizes)
- Clear packaging tape
- Spray adhesive
- Double-sided tape

- Highlighter
- Scissors
- Pen/pencil
- Waxed paper
- Wood finish (I use a clear gel varnish)
- Paper towels
- Disposable foam or glue brush
- Latex or nitrile gloves
- Black permanent marker
- Rubber bumpers (optional)

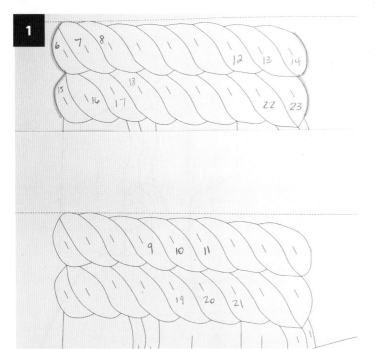

1 **Number the pattern pieces.** Start with five copies of the pattern plus the master to place your pieces onto. Number the pieces on the master pattern, particularly the rope pieces, as they'll be hard to keep track of otherwise. Number the pattern pieces on the other copies so that no pieces are adjoining another piece that will be cut out. The exception to this is the rope. You can cut the rope pieces in groups of three or four. Avoid cutting all of them together, as some of the kerf is lost with each cut, which would cause you to end up with a segment of rope that is too short to fit properly, with larger-than-desired gaps between each piece. The rope areas that are not inset into other pieces (bottom left and segment under right buoy) can be cut together from one piece. Once you have numbered all the pieces, highlight the outer edges of the pattern pieces that will be cut out and applied to your wood. This will indicate when cutting that no pieces adjoin them, so if you stray off the line, the fit won't be affected.

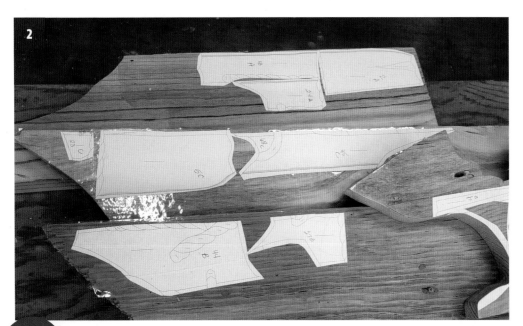

2 **Cut out the pattern pieces and affix to the wood.** Apply clear packaging tape to the wood. Using spray adhesive, apply the pattern pieces utilizing the most appropriate grain for that piece. When using assorted shades of the same wood type, it helps to label them on the master pattern so you can easily identify which shades are for which pieces. A,B,C or L,M,D (light, medium, dark) are useful indicators. If needed, cut the boards into manageable sizes that can be handled on your scroll saw. You can cut all the project pieces at once or break it down into segments as I did.

TIP

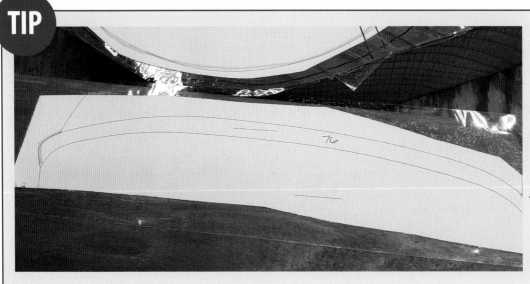

When cutting long and narrow pattern pieces out, such as the middle piece of the round buoy, leave the paper pattern piece larger and wider. This will avoid distortion when you apply it to the wood. A narrow piece such as this can easily "bend" slightly due to the weight of the adhesive and the piece will not fit properly.

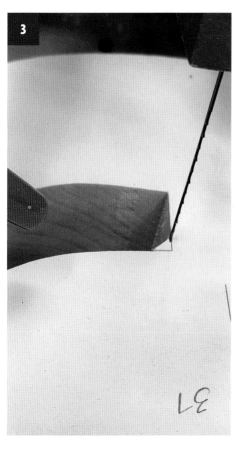

3 **Cut out the buoy pieces.** When cutting out the markings on the left buoy, you want your corners to be sharp so the inset pieces will fit well. Curve around the corners on your first pass and remove the waste. Go back from the other direction and cut out each corner. For most of this project, I used Pegas Modified Geometry #7 blades. For more instruction, consult the Basic Steps of Intarsia section on page 13.

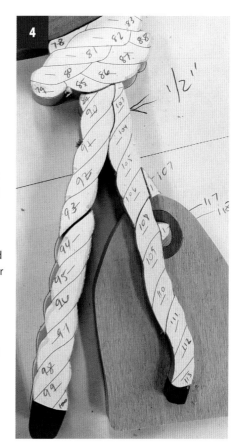

4 **Cut out the rope pieces.** When cutting out the rope pieces, an easy way to ensure crisp cuts is to skip over the sharp corners, then go back from the other direction to complete. Do not separate any of the individual rope pieces until you are ready to shape them.

5 **Shape the fence post and attach fence pieces to the shim.** You will want to sand it down to roughly ½" (1.3cm) thick so the buoys will stand proud. Using a sanding shim of roughly ¼" x 4" x 12" (6.4 x 101.6 x 304.8mm) plywood, lay out the pieces of the fence post in the orientation they appear in the pattern (all "A" pieces to the left, "B" pieces in the center, and "C" pieces on the right). Attach the pieces to the sanding shim with two-sided, pressure-sensitive turner's tape.

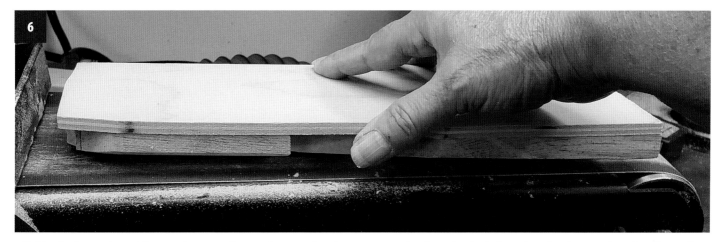

6 **Thin the fence pieces.** Thinning the pieces down and curving the edges is more easily achieved with a belt sander. A flex drum sander will work as well, but it may take a bit longer. As you thin the pieces, gently roll the shim to each side of the sander, tapering the outer edges to a gentle curve.

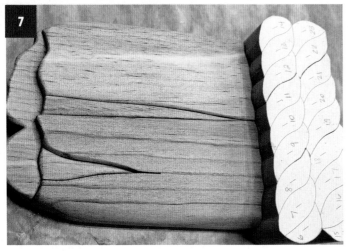

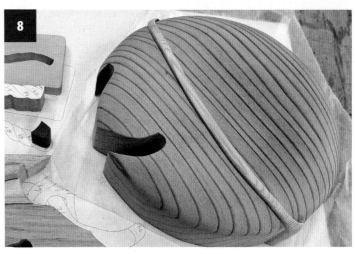

7 **Sand with the flex drum sander.** Finish off sanding the pieces with the flex drum sander in the direction of the grain. Remove the two-sided tape with a paring knife by sliding it under the piece and popping it off. Reassemble the pieces on the master pattern. Taper the very top post piece inward at the bottom so it gives the appearance of the top of a rounded post. Inset the two smaller pieces slightly to add dimension. For more shaping instructions, see the Introduction to Shaping section (page 22).

8 **Shape the buoys.** Use a sanding shim as you did for the fence when shaping the round buoy's two large pieces. Shape, then insert the middle piece and sand it to about ⅛" (3.2mm) thicker than the other pieces. For the other two buoys, glue the segments of each together and allow to dry. Shape each as one piece, contouring the outer edges. The left one should end up slightly higher than the right.

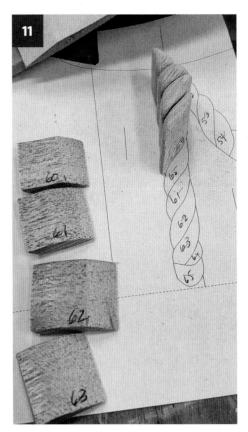

9 **Separate the rope pieces.** Using a #2 or #3 blade, separate the rope pieces and number the bottom of each piece. For the smaller ropes, put a piece of scrap plywood under the sections while cutting to keep them from falling through the hole of the scroll saw.

10 **Shape the rope pieces.** The larger top and lower left rope pieces can be shaped with the flex drum sander first. Slightly round over each side of a piece. Align the next piece to it and draw a line as a reference for where you should sand.

11 **Soften the edges.** Hand sand around all the edges to soften and align the pieces. Once you get to the smallest rope pieces, I found it easiest to hand sand each piece individually and glue them together as I went along.

12

TIP

Add Some Flare

For an interesting challenge, you might consider using real rope instead. This would add a whole new element to the finished piece! For a little extra flare, distressing the fence post would add to the already weathered look of it.

13

12 **Add risers, if needed.** Because of the thickness of the wood I chose, I utilized a ¼" (6.4mm) riser under the rope on the left buoy. You might not need one for thicker wood. Continue to follow all shaping guidelines as laid out in the Introduction to Shaping section (page 22).

13 **Glue the project and apply finish.** Follow all the usual steps for glue-up and finishing. Note: Because the right rope attached to the tag is such a delicate area, glue this segment to the buoy after the finish has been applied and is allowed to dry. It is likely to break off during finishing otherwise.

14

14 **Cut out backer and adhere it to the project, then attach the hanger.** Follow all the usual steps for cutting out your backer and affixing it to the project. Be sure to clean up any glue overflow. Once dried, attach your hanger. For more detailed instructions, see the Basic Steps of Intarsia (page 13).

I know very little about classic cars, but I do have a great appreciation for them. This design was inspired by an old photo I found of my parents from before I was born. I'd like to share my dad's story about his car. He calls it "Best Trade Ever." I hope you enjoy it as much as I did.

TOOLS AND MATERIALS

Note: Listed here are the woods I used. I encourage you to get creative and use what you have on hand or can get easily. These wood sizes are only approximate. The size you need can vary greatly depending on how you orient the pattern pieces on the wood. I always recommend having larger pieces to give you greater options.

- Aromatic red cedar, 1" (2.5cm) thick and a minimum of 6" (16.2cm) wide; be sure the wood is clear of knots
- Blue pine, several shades
- Peruvian walnut, 1" (2.5cm) thick
- Aspen, 1" (2.5cm) thick
- Curly maple, ¼"–⁵⁄₁₆" (6.4–7.9mm) thick
- ⅛" x 18" x 10 ½" (3.2 x 457.2 x 266.7mm) Baltic birch plywood (for backer)
- Scroll saw

- Scroll saw blades (check instructions for specific sizes)
- Belt sander
- Sanding mop
- Sandpaper, 220 grit
- Sanding sponge or sanding block
- Spindle sander
- Flex drum sander
- Rotary tool and assorted burrs (check instructions for specific types)
- Wood glue
- Skewer
- Utility knife

- CA glue
- Air compressor
- Sharp dental tool
- Rubber-tipped dental tool
- Awl
- Carbon or graphite paper
- L-clamps (however many needed to apply even pressure all over)
- Soft cloths or old socks
- Hanger kit
- Drill or drill press and assorted bits (check instructions for specific sizes)

- Clear packaging tape
- Spray adhesive
- Double-sided tape
- Highlighter
- Scissors
- Pen/pencil
- Waxed paper
- Wood finish (I use a clear gel varnish)
- Paper towels
- Disposable foam or glue brush
- Latex or nitrile gloves
- Black permanent marker
- Rubber bumpers (optional)

Best Trade Ever

Back in the day, I was not the sane, serious, sober-sided person I am now. One of my first "real" jobs was working as a bank teller for $50.00 a week ($42.50 after taxes). So, my treat to myself for putting up with the regimentation of banking was to buy a brand new, fire-engine-red 1960 MGA convertible roadster. It had two leather seats and a trunk that would hold the spare tire and a six pack. There was a compartment between the seats that would hold a pair of pliers and a pack of cigarettes. That was where the fuel pump was located. I could never figure out why the fuel pump was there—until the first time the engine started to sputter and die. The dealer explained to me that Morris Garage couldn't figure out how to make a decent fuel pump, so they put this compartment in so you could lift the top and give it a gentle tap when needed. As a single young guy, I put many happy miles on this car. When the guys with the Chevys and Fords were showing off the eight-cylinder engines in their cars, my dinky four banger was kept hidden under the well-polished hood. After many miles and gentle taps, I met my soon-to-be bride. We drove the car all over the east coast and part of Eastern Canada. Well, as it often does, nature took its course, and although my two-seater carried three full-sized adults on many occasions, it was time to get an ordinary car with room for an infant and her attendant gear. I often think back to the fun associated with that car. But, if I had kept it, it would now have over two million miles on it. The prize from that trade-in, however, has turned out to be priceless.—Fred Prout

The big lesson for this project is the perspective aspect of the design. It can seem daunting at first, trying to decide where to thin pieces or add risers. Slight tapering of strategic areas creates the right illusion and proportions. Wood thickness comes into play in the dimensionality, as does the use of risers. The angle of the car creates much of the perspective itself. The shaping adds to this. Perspective gives a three-dimensional feeling to a flat image. For intarsia purposes, just remember thicker is closer and thinner is farther away. Creating the contour and texture of the bumper provides good practice in shaping, adding interest to the overall piece.

1 Prepare pattern, select your woods, and apply the pattern pieces. You will need five copies of the pattern, plus a master copy. As usual, cover the wood with clear packaging tape before coating with an adhesive spray and applying the pattern pieces.

2 Drill the holes. Drill the nine holes where pieces will be inserted: two in the outer grill piece, two in the red pieces for the fog lights, two in the gray rim of the fog lights for the light insert, one in each of the dark tire centers, and one in the gray area of the front tire. I suggest using a ⅛" (3.2mm) brad point bit. Place a scrap piece under the workpiece when drilling to avoid tear out. Alternatively, set the drill press so just the point of the bit comes through the bottom of the piece, then flip the piece over to complete the hole. This produces a clean hole.

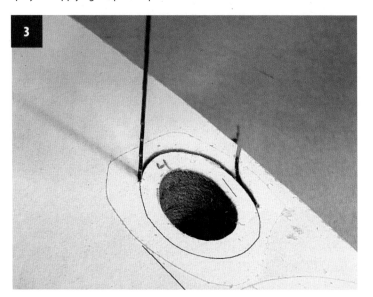

3 Cut out the drilled pieces. Cut out the drilled areas before cutting the perimeter of the pieces. It's easier to handle larger pieces. When cutting out the center of the lights, insert the blade into the hole, cut towards the edge, and turn clockwise. Cut a short distance and back the blade out. Rotate the piece and feed the blade backwards into the kerf you just cut. Cut counterclockwise around the perimeter, following the line closely to complete the cut. Cut the infill pieces in the same manner. This method is optional, but I find it works best when cutting out smaller circles that will receive inlay pieces. Cut the perimeter of the car seat pieces, then switch to a finer #3 blade to separate the individual pieces.

4 Finish cutting and assemble. Cut out remaining pieces and assemble the project on the master pattern. Make any minor fit adjustments if needed.

5 **Cut out the risers.** Some areas may need risers, depending on the thickness of the wood you started with. The right front panel should be raised ⅛" (3.2mm) above the hood. Glue this riser into place. The chrome bumper, headlights, and front grill should all sit higher than the body parts. Don't attach these risers until shaping is completed in case adjustments are needed.

TIP For shaping guidance, refer to the angle and side photos of the finished project. For the perspective aspect of the project, an easy rule to keep in mind is everything to the right of the right headlight is tapered to the right, and everything to the left is tapered to the left.

6 **Shape the chassis.** Start by shaping the hood. The side where the hood meets the windshield should be slightly lower than the front. The entire piece is tapered downward toward the front and to the left toward the windshield. Slightly curve the sides where they meet the front quarter panels. Then, shape the front quarter panel to the left of the hood. Draw a light line to indicate where it meets the hod. The right side should taper down to gradually disappear behind the hood piece. Keep the left side slightly higher than the hood and round it down to where they meet. Finally, shape the right front quarter panel and driver's door. These are best shaped together. Using double-sided tape, attach the pieces to a sanding shim that is ¼" (6.4mm) thick. Be sure the riser for the quarter panel is glued on. It will sit ⅛" (3.2mm) higher than the driver's door. Sand the pieces together, tapering them lower toward the back of the car. The two pieces should blend smoothly where they meet. Round the front quarter panel to meet the hood. This piece should be higher than the hood by about ¼" (6.4mm) at the front. Shape the rocker panel below at the same angle, and round over the bottom slightly.

7 **Shape the windshield and its frame.** Draw a pencil line along the windshield frame piece where it meets the hood. Taper this piece along the drawn line, leaving it about 1⁄16" (1.6mm) higher than the hood. The right side should be slightly lower than the side panel so it appears to disappear behind it. Angle the entire piece back slightly where it meets the windshield. Shape the bottom of the windshield to follow the contour of the lower frame piece from side to side. Overall, it should sit slightly lower than the frame. Taper the piece downward from bottom to top. The top will be lower and the top left side slightly lower still. Then, shape the windshield frame. Taper the top and side windshield frame pieces to follow the contour of the windshield, leaving them slightly higher.

8 **Shape the tires.** The tires should be shaped to taper toward the right slightly.

9 **Shape the bumper and add indents.** Roughly shape the contour of the bumper to follow the line of the hood. Add risers as needed. The bumper should be higher than the front tire and the hood. With a rotary tool sanding bit, create two indents in each bumper piece.

10 **Smooth the bumpers.** Fine tune and smooth with a rounded profile sander.

11 **Shape the seat.** Rough shape the back of the car seat first. Draw a line where the seat back pieces meet to use as a guide. It's easier to shape these small pieces if you make a sacrificial frame to contain them while shaping. This will ensure they are all uniform. Using a piece of pine or other soft scrap wood, cut out the shape of the seat and insert the seat pieces. Attach the seat pieces and the frame to a sanding shim with two-sided tape. Once the desired height and angle is achieved, remove the pieces and hand sand each one individually. Each piece should be slightly rounded over to give the appearance of tufted leather.

12 **Shape the remaining pieces.** The grill pieces should follow the same contour of the hood. Rough shape the three pieces together with a sanding shim, then sand the two inner pieces slightly lower. The outer grill piece should sit slightly higher than the hood. The wheel well pieces are tapered down and to the left to add depth behind the tires. The back quarter panel beside the seat is rounded over to give it a bubble-like appearance, keeping the rim where it meets the wheel well sharp. It should sit just higher than the seat. The lights should sit just above their rims and are rounded down to meet the rim. The light and rims sit just higher than the car body. Reduce the thickness of the front tire on the left to sit below the valance under the bumper. The bumper guards should be higher than the bumper.

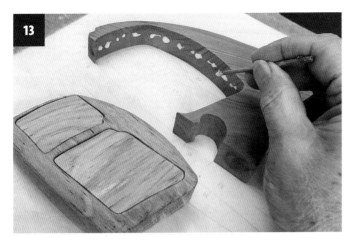

13 **Glue your project.** Glue the risers to their respective pieces. I glued smaller areas together in segments. I find it's easier to assemble this way when working with small pieces. Reassemble the entire project often to ensure everything still fits together well. I glued the tires, windshield, grill pieces, and seat assembly. Once these are dry, complete the gluing.

14 **Apply the finish.** Use your finish of choice and be sure to wipe away any excess. For more finishing instructions, see the Basic Steps of Intarsia section (page 13).

15 **Cut out the backer.** Trace the project onto the backer and cut it out. Remember to apply black marker around the backer edges to make it less noticeable, if desired.

16 **Apply the backer and hanger.** Glue the backer to project and clamp. Once dry, apply the hanger and enjoy!

Oregon Lighthouse

Advanced

Pattern on pages 128–133

The Heceta Head Lighthouse has been a working lighthouse in Lane County, Oregon since its lens was first lit in 1894. It is an iconic part of the Oregon coast and one of the most photographed lighthouses in the United States. One of eleven lighthouses along the Oregon coast, it keeps the fishermen safe from the rocky shoreline and is a major attraction for tourists and photographers from around the world. The lighthouse keeper's house is a bed and breakfast, famous for their quaint (and possibly haunted) rooms and seven-course brunch. We had the pleasure of staying there once years ago and had a wonderful time.

In this project, you will create depth by varying the thickness of the woods. By thinning down some and adding varying heights of risers to others, this becomes a very dimensional project. Thinner pieces represent the background farther way and get thicker the closer to the foreground you get, ending at the thickest, lowest piece on the bottom. Perspective is enhanced in both the angle of the buildings and the varying depths created. Working methodically with tiny pieces will build your patience and organizational skills. Creating a frame for this project adds a level of completeness and enhances the overall look.

TOOLS AND MATERIALS

Note: Listed here are the woods I used. I encourage you to get creative and use what you have on hand or can get easily. These wood sizes are only approximate. The size you need can vary greatly depending on how you orient the pattern pieces on the wood. I always recommend having larger pieces to give you greater options.

- Baltic birch plywood scraps, ⅛"–½" (1.6–12.7mm)
- Green poplar, varying shades (for foreground)
- Yellowheart, 1" (2.5cm) thick (for the light)
- Redwood, 1½" x 2" x 6" (3.8 x 5.1 x 15.2cm); used for frame
- Maple, 1" (2.5cm) thick (for buildings and lighthouse)
- Blue pine ¾" (1.9cm) thick (for sky, water, and buildings)
- Aspen, ½" (1.3cm) thick (for clouds)
- Red cedar, 1" (2.5cm) thick (for roof)

- Walnut scraps (for windows and doors)
- Spalted and burly maple scraps (for shrubs)
- Quarter-sawn red sycamore (for land)
- Scroll saw
- Scroll saw blades (check instructions for specific sizes)
- Belt sander
- Sanding mop
- Sandpaper, 220 grit
- Sanding sponge or sanding block
- Spindle sander
- Flex drum sander
- Rotary tool and assorted burrs (check instructions for specific types)

- Wood glue
- Skewer
- Utility knife
- CA glue
- Air compressor
- Sharp dental tool
- Rubber-tipped dental tool
- Awl
- Carbon or graphite paper
- L-clamps (however many needed to apply even pressure all over)
- Soft cloths or old socks
- Hanger kit
- Drill or drill press and assorted bits

- (check instructions for specific sizes)
- Clear packaging tape
- Spray adhesive
- Double-sided tape
- Highlighter
- Scissors
- Pen/pencil
- Waxed paper
- Wood finish (I use a clear gel varnish)
- Paper towels
- Disposable foam or glue brush
- Latex or nitrile gloves
- Black permanent marker
- Rubber bumpers (optional)

1 **Prepare the pattern and sand the wood for the frame.** Prepare the pattern as usual, then sand the wood for the frame. Sanding the wood before cutting will save time and be easier in the long run. Start with 180-grit sandpaper, followed by 220-grit with a random orbital sander or your sander of choice.

2 **Apply the pattern pieces, then cut.** Apply packaging tape to the wood, then apply the frame pattern pieces. Cut the pieces and dry fit them together. Label the backs of the pieces.

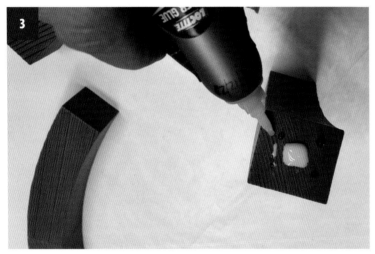

3 **Soften the edges and glue the frame together.** Soften the edges with sandpaper and go over all sides with the sanding mop. I used both wood glue for strength and CA glue for a quick bond. Allow the frame to dry thoroughly.

TIP
Shaping the Background

Because the wood I used for the background was ¾" (1.9cm) stock, it had to be thinned down. If you have a planer, you can simply plane the wood for the sky and water to ⅜" (9.5mm) thick. To resaw on the bandsaw, follow these steps. If using a planer, you can skip ahead to step 4, just be sure to cut out all your background pieces first.

To thin your wood down, first lay out the pattern pieces onto the wood and draw a pencil line around them to indicate the rough size of the wood to you'll be using. Lay them out so that the ones on the left side of the lighthouse are beside the continuation pieces from the right side. Cut out these segments with the bandsaw or scroll saw, keeping a straight edge along the bottom to make it safer and easier to resaw. Prepare all water and sky wood pieces this way so you end up with workable sizes that will fit your bandsaw height.

4 **Adhere the pattern, then cut out the sky and water pieces.** Apply packaging tape, then adhere the pattern to the wood. Using a #3 reverse tooth blade, cut out the sky and water pieces and dry fit into the frame.

5 Cut out the clouds. The clouds are ½" (1.3cm) aspen. Resaw in the same manner as the sky and water, if needed (see sidebar on page 90). You want them to sit about ⅛" (3.2mm) higher than the sky pieces. Cut out the cloud pieces.

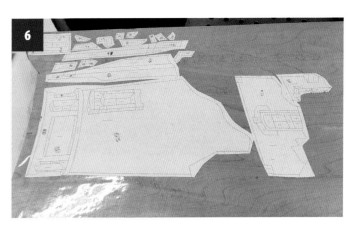

6 Cut out and apply white pattern pieces. Cut out the white pattern pieces for the lighthouse and buildings. In areas of doors and windows where the grain direction is the same, keep these pattern pieces together. Apply to the wood.

7 Cut out the small wood pieces. Cut the smaller pieces out first. To avoid losing them through the hole in the saw table, cut out three sides of the small piece, then put a scrap piece of ⅛" (3.2mm) plywood underneath to cover the hole in the scroll saw table for the final cut. Alternatively, you can apply blue painter's tape over the hole. I find it handy to keep a small box beside my saw to put the pieces into as they are cut out.

8 Cut out window and large lighthouse pieces. Drill a blade entry hole into the lighthouse window and cut it out, then cut the perimeter of the larger lighthouse pieces.

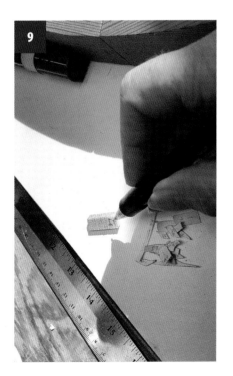

9 Cut out the remaining pieces. Cut the remaining pieces out and remove the fuzzies from the bottom of the larger pieces. As you remove each pattern piece, transfer the number to the bottom of the piece. For the smaller pieces, using the side might be easier. Be sure to indicate which direction faces the top so you don't inadvertently assemble it facing the wrong way.

10 Assemble the project. Assemble the project within the frame, making fit adjustments as needed. It's easiest to insert the main pieces first, then the small window pieces.

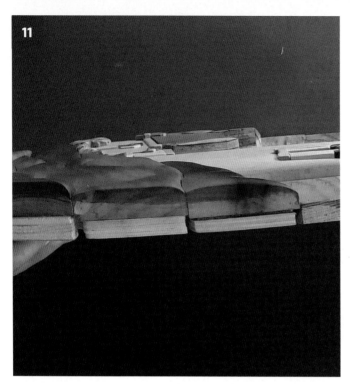

11 **Add risers where needed.** Remember, the thickness of the risers will vary depending on the thickness of the pieces you've cut out. This photo shows the edge view of the finished piece without the frame. Start with the foreground pieces. The piece on the right that meets the water was raised 5/16" (7.9mm). It was about 5/8" (1.6cm) thick to start with. This brings the height up to just shy of 1" (2.5cm) in total. The very bottom right piece was raised to a final height of 1¼" (3.2cm), and the rest of the green pieces are about 1/8" (3.2mm) shorter. Cut out and dry fit all the risers and adjust until the desired heights are reached. If you need to double up on risers, apply double-sided tape to the two thicknesses and cut them out together. Don't forget to remove the tape and glue the risers together afterward.

12 **Glue risers to pieces.** Glue the foreground pieces to the risers and clamp until dry.

13 **Shape the clouds.** Since the clouds are pretty thin to begin with, add some contouring within them for extra interest. I used a ball-shaped burr in my rotary tool, followed by the flex drum sander to remove the scratches. Round over the edges of the clouds down to meet the sky pieces by hand. The outer cloud pieces should appear to be in front of the inner pieces.

14 **Glue the background.** Soften the edges of the sky and water pieces and glue the background pieces together.

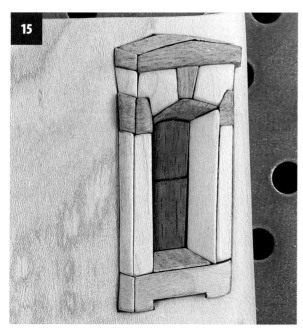

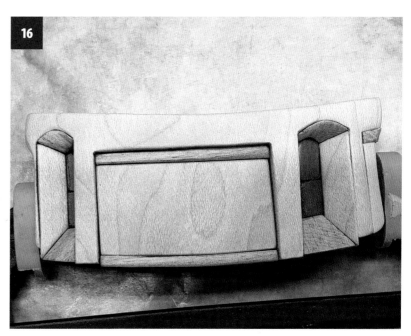

15 **Contour the larger lighthouse pieces.** For the upper portion, I shaped the larger piece with the window pieces in place using a sanding shim. This way, I could ensure that everything was the same contour. If necessary, add a ⅛" (3.2mm) riser the size of the window and shape the individual window pieces. The dark windowpanes should sit lower into the window and the right side should taper down toward them. The lower gray window ledge should taper back toward the windowpanes. The outer frame sits slightly higher than the lighthouse body. Glue the window pieces to the riser and to the lighthouse body.

16 **Continue shaping the lighthouse.** Moving up the lighthouse, shape and glue the windows for the next section in the same manner as the previous step.

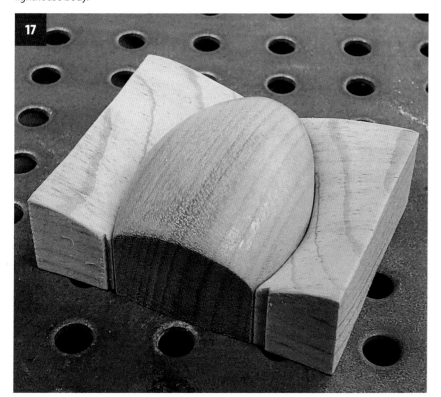

17 **Shape the light.** Contour the pieces beside the light downward toward the center so that they appear to go behind the light. Shape the light. The top and bottom should sit lower than adjoining pieces. Sides should meet the contoured adjoining edges.

18 **Continue shaping the lighthouse.** Continue your way up until the entire lighthouse is shaped. Keep the gray cross pieces slightly higher than the main white pieces to add extra relief. Be sure to add a matching curve to these as well. Taper the red roof back slightly.

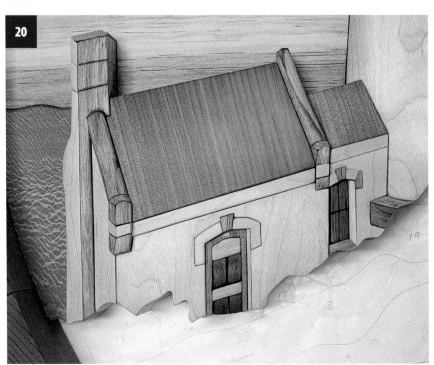

19 **Glue the lighthouse.** Glue the lighthouse pieces together and to the background pieces.

20 **Shape the lighthouse building.** The right side of the small building should sit slightly higher than the lighthouse. Taper the top of the red roof back. The red roof and cross piece beneath it should sit slightly higher than the front of the building. The trim work around the doors sits slightly higher as well. This adds depth and some relief to the overall look of the project. The walnut part of the doors is inset and the right side tapers down to meet it. I added a ⅛" (3.2mm) riser to the left red roof and cross piece beneath it so that this part of the building appears closer. The gray "beams" beside the roof sit higher by ⅛" (3.2mm). Sand all the pieces and glue them together.

21 **Contour the foreground.** The green foreground pieces add a lot of depth to the overall project. Besides varying the height, I wanted to add contour to each piece. The rotary tool with a flame point burr is perfect for this. It allows you to add dips and waves into the inner areas of each piece. Begin with the top right piece and add desired contour to it. Smooth out the scratches and refine the shaping with the flex drum sander before moving on to an adjacent piece. By removing some material on the bottom of a piece, it will make the next piece beneath it appear even higher. Mark the next piece with a pencil as a guide for shaping. Repeat the process. Round over the top of the pieces, rather than shape to the line. This gives the impression that the piece is higher than the one above it. Between this and thinning the lower part of the piece, you create the illusion of added depth.

22 **Shape the bushes.** I saved these until last so I could make the necessary height adjustments while shaping. They should appear to be in front of the buildings and behind the foreground. They will sit higher than the building and about the same height as the foreground. Add some contour to these pieces, round over the edges to meet the surrounding pieces. Then reassemble and glue the project pieces.

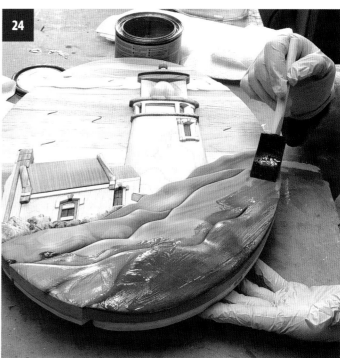

23 **Reassemble the project and finish the frame.** Apply finish to the frame on three sides. Remove excess and wipe thoroughly with clean towels. Reassemble the pieces and glue into place one at a time, ensuring they continue to fit well as you go. I chose not to glue the project to the frame. It's easier to finish the frame separately, then glue both to a backer once the finish has dried.

24 **Finish the foreground.** Finish the main portion in sections so the finish doesn't dry out before you get a chance to remove it from the cracks. Starting in the foreground, apply finish to the green areas. Wipe off excess and blow out any excess from the cracks with an air compressor. Be sure to protect the rest of the piece from excess splatter.

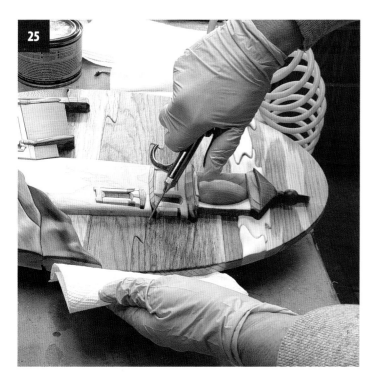

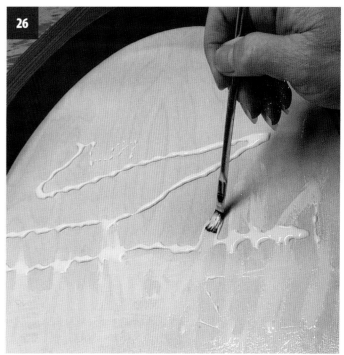

25 **Finish the background, then remove the excess.** Work your way around the project in sections until complete. Examine the entire project closely to ensure that all excess finish has been removed. Allow to dry thoroughly overnight and apply a second coat.

26 **Make the backer, adhere the project, and attach the hanger.** Because this project is pretty sturdy, ⅛" (3.2mm) ply should suffice for the backer, but feel free to go thicker. Trace the frame onto the backer material and mark which end is up. Apply glue to the back of the frame and glue the backer to it. Clamp until dry. Then, apply glue to the inner part of the frame and insert the project into it. Place weight on top until the glue dries. Follow all usual steps for adhering the backer.

Wood Duck on a Branch

Advanced

Pattern on pages 122–127

Years ago, I came across a photo of a flying tufted puffin in a coastal Oregon newspaper. I had never seen a puffin in flight before and loved the photo. I contacted the photographer, Ram Papish, and asked if I could use his photo to create an intarsia pattern. The cost was a compound-cut birdhouse ornament! When I decided to create a wood duck design for this book, I was reminded of his amazing photos and found the perfect one. Ram was once again gracious enough to allow me to use it for my intarsia project. Wood ducks are colorful birds, found throughout many areas of North America. If you are lucky enough to spot one, you are sure to be entranced by the male's beautiful plumage.

Cutting the pieces for this project is straightforward. Refining your cutting skills will be important because the pieces need to flow seamlessly from one to the next in the head and body of the duck. Gaps will be more visible in areas like this where multiple pieces act as shading and are shaped as one piece. Sanding shims are utilized for much of this project. There are multiple areas that are shaped as one piece initially to produce the overall shape of the duck. This helps you to create a cohesive flow throughout the body. After rough shaping, pieces are refined individually. Risers are used to bring up the height of some pieces where needed. You will get good hands-on practice mixing dyes to produce the desired colors for various pieces. It's important to test the colors out on scrap wood that is the same as the wood you use for the actual pieces. Another challenge with this project is working with and handling small pieces.

TOOLS AND MATERIALS

Note: Listed here are the woods I used. I encourage you to get creative and use what you have on hand or can get easily. These wood sizes are only approximate. The size you need can vary greatly depending on how you orient the pattern pieces on the wood. I always recommend having larger pieces to give you more options. All the head pieces are a minimum of ¾" (1.9cm) thick, and the body pieces are ⅞"–1" (2.2–2.5cm) thick overall.

- Peruvian walnut; used for the darkest pieces
- Figured walnut; used for some of the feathers
- Buckeye burl; used for dark gray areas
- Aspen; used for white areas (dyed aspen is used for blue tailfeathers)
- Sycamore, various shades; used for main body parts
- Purpleheart; used for purple areas
- Juniper, two shades; used for beak, eye, and feet
- Ebony; used for pupil
- Curly maple and hard maple; used for dyed pieces

- Spalted maple burl; used for branch
- Walnut; used for branch
- Baltic birch plywood, ⅛" (3.2mm); used for backer
- Scrap ¼" pieces of plywood (large)
- Wood dye (powder, water-based paints, stains or tinted finishes, etc.)
- Scroll saw
- Scroll saw blades (check instructions for specific sizes)
- Belt sander
- Sanding mop
- Sandpaper, 220 grit
- Sanding sponge or sanding block

- Spindle sander
- Flex drum sander
- Rotary tool and assorted burrs (check instructions for specific types)
- Wood glue
- Skewer
- Utility knife
- CA glue
- Air compressor
- Sharp dental tool
- Rubber-tipped dental tool
- Awl
- Carbon or graphite paper
- L-clamps (however many needed to apply even pressure all over)
- Soft cloths or old socks
- Hanger kit

- Drill or drill press and assorted bits (check instructions for specific sizes)
- Clear packaging tape
- Spray adhesive
- Double-sided tape
- Highlighter
- Scissors
- Pen/pencil
- Waxed paper
- Wood finish (I use a clear gel varnish)
- Paper towels
- Disposable foam or glue brush
- Latex or nitrile gloves
- Black permanent marker
- Rubber bumpers (optional)

Practicing with Dyes

Before I even started the project, I experimented with the dyes to come up with the final colors needed and decide which woods were potential candidates for the dyed pieces. Gather some empty jars with lids to mix your colors. Get some scrap pieces of assorted shades of sycamore, hard maple, curly maple, and aspen, or whatever woods you plan to use. Following the package directions, mix up a small amount of the royal blue. I liked this shade of blue on its own for the duck's feathers and experimented with different dilutions for the lighter and darker shades. Apply a small amount on each scrap of wood. You can add additional coats to darken, or increase the amount of dye in the mix. In a separate jar, mix up some yellow. Transfer some of the blue to another jar and save for the blue feathers. Add a very small amount of yellow to the blue to produce the teal shade. Experiment with the colors until the desired shade is reached. When using dyes, I recommend having lots of paper towels on-hand. Use gloves and protect the surface area you're working on. Also, don't leave open jars of dye unattended (especially if you have cats).

1 Prepare the pattern and cut out the pieces. You will need six copies of the pattern and an extra for the master copy. Prepare the pieces as directed in the Basic Steps of Intarsia section (page 13), numbering the pieces and highlighting the outlines of the outside areas. Select the woods you will use and apply the pattern pieces. Then, cut out the pieces following the usual steps.

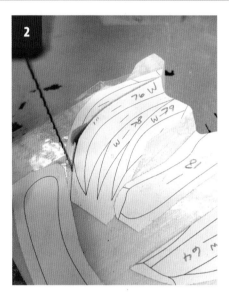

2 Cut out the small, feathered areas. When working with the small dark and white feather areas, it's easier to cut one larger pattern piece for several of one color, then cut out the individual pieces from it.

3 Cut out the beak and tailfeathers. For the beak, cut the two juniper pieces out together, then switch to a #3 blade to separate them. Do this for the dark tail feathers as well.

4 Cut the pieces that will be dyed. I cut the pieces that were to be dyed last to make it easier to keep track of them. As you peel off the pattern, be sure to number the bottom and note what color it will be. This will make things a lot easier later. I also kept the pattern pieces grouped together by color once I peeled them off, as this gave me a way to quickly reference them. Assemble all the pieces and adjust the fit as necessary.

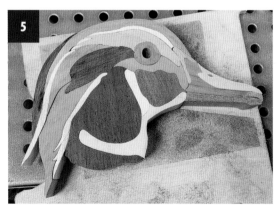

5 Shape the head. For best results shaping this project, I used a series of sanding shims to shape different areas together. Beginning with the head, use two-sided tape and assemble the head pieces on a ¼" (6.4mm) sanding shim.

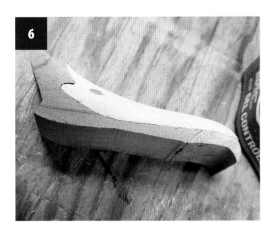

6 **Shape the beak.** Use a flame point burr to shape the duck's beak. A paring knife is ideal for popping the pieces off the sanding shim once done. Simply slide the blade under the piece and twist it. Smooth out the scratches, then hand sand the individual pieces. Finally, glue the beak pieces together.

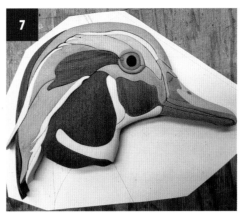

7 **Cut out and sand the eye and assemble head pieces.** The outer eye pieces should be about 1/16" (1.6mm) higher than the rest of the head pieces. Hand sand the outer eye pieces to round over both the inner and outer sides. The pupil pieces should be slightly lower than the outer rim. Once finished, sand, dry fit, and set aside all the head pieces.

TIP Many of the pieces have narrow ends that come to a point. Be careful not to accidentally over sand these ends. Thinner areas like this will sand much more quickly than the rest of the piece, and you could end up sanding off too much. Use a light touch and pay close attention when shaping these areas. If this happens on an inner piece, add a riser to the piece and reshape.

8 **Shape the body pieces.** Use a shim to rough shape the neck and chest pieces first, rounding over and contouring the chest and back of the neck. Smooth with the 220-grit flex drum sander, then remove the pieces from the sanding shim. Then, align the chest and belly pieces and draw the reference line for shaping the belly. Shape the belly pieces, tapering slightly lower toward the back of the duck. Round over the belly pieces, being careful not to round too far where the leg pieces join the body. Reassemble the pieces.

9 **Assemble the dark tailfeathers.** For all the feathers in this project, you want them to follow the contour of the body, yet subtly stand out on their own. You can achieve this by sanding pieces as a group, then going back to individual pieces to adjust slightly so they stand out on their own. Assemble the dark tailfeather pieces along with the two other pieces to the right on a sanding shim. Taper the feathers downward so that the back end on the left ends up at about 1/2" (1.3cm) thick.

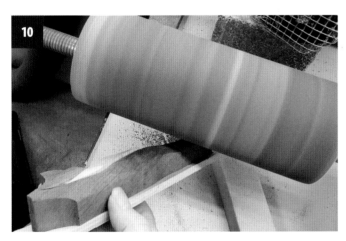

10 **Round over the top of the entire segment.** Then, go back and hand sand each feather piece so it ends up sitting slightly below the previous one. Refer to the photos of the finished project for guidance.

11 **Repeat the process on upper tailfeathers.** Assemble the upper tailfeather pieces on sanding shim and do the same as in steps 9 and 10.

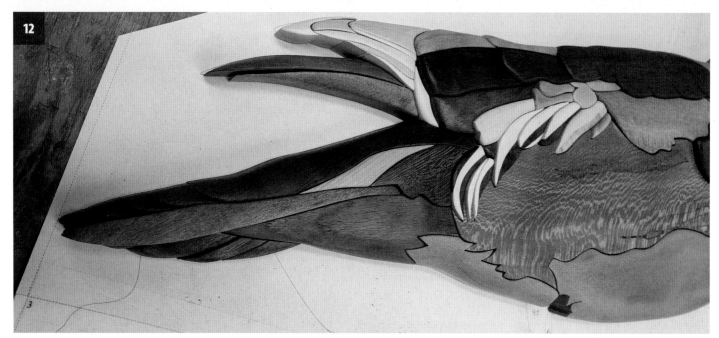

12 **Shape the remaining feathers.** For the small dark and white curved feathers in the midsection, glue the dark and white segments of each feather together and allow them to dry. You will end up with six segments plus two single pieces. Contour these pieces inward slightly to the right, staying above the main body piece they fit into. By shaping the right side of each piece downward, definition is added, yet they remain in line with the overall contour of the body. Feathers on a duck generally sit tight to the body. Remember, you want them to blend in, yet subtly stand out individually.

13 **Shape the branch.** Shape the branch by rounding over the bottom, adding dips, and contouring with the flex drum and spindle sanders. Taper the left side where it attaches to the tailfeathers down so that it sits below the feathers. This may need to be sanded down to ¼" (6.4mm) depending on the height of feathers. Dry fit the entire project, making shaping adjustments as needed.

14 **Glue the body pieces.** Glue the majority of the body pieces together except the feather pieces that will be dyed. Use these pieces as placeholders to ensure everything fits properly, but don't glue in place.

TIP

Pay attention to the sides of pieces you're dying. Refer to the pattern if you're unsure if the edge of a piece will be visible or not once glued. I had the entire project finished and glued before noticing that one small, exposed edge of one of the pieces hadn't been dyed. I spent some time with a sharpened skewer and dye, dabbing it delicately to avoid the white piece adjoining it.

15 **Dye the pieces.** There are 16 pieces that need to be dyed. Sort the pieces into the colors you plan to dye them. Apply the dye with a disposable brush, adding multiple coats as needed until the desired color is reached. If the grain rises, sand lightly with the sanding mop after they have thoroughly dried.

16 Apply tape. Apply small amounts of painter's tape to the edges of the pieces yet to be glued. Refer to the pattern to ensure only the inside edges are taped. This will keep the finish off areas that will receive glue and ensure better adhesion.

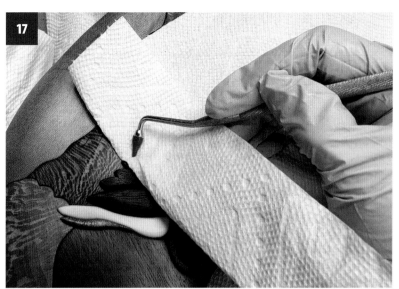

17 Apply the finish and remove excess. Apply finish with a disposable foam brush to the main body. Remove as much excess finish as possible with paper towels. Use an air compressor to remove any finish from the cracks and hard-to-reach areas. Go around each piece with a rubber tipped dental tool to remove any finish that remains. Finish the unglued pieces individually. Allow to dry thoroughly and apply a second coat. The dyed pieces may bleed, so finish them last. Once done, remove all the tape from the edges and glue the rest of the pieces in place. Allow to dry overnight.

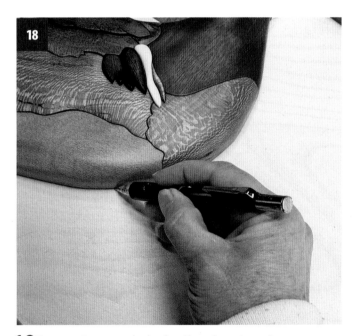

18 Trace project onto the backer. Trace the entire project onto ⅛" (3.2mm) the Baltic birch plywood backer. Graphite paper and an awl are handy to get into narrow areas a pencil tip won't reach. Drill a hole in the waste area between the duck and the log.

19 Cut out the backer and adhere it to the project, then attach the hanger. Follow the usual steps and apply your hanger once finished.

Carousel Horse

Advanced

Pattern on pages 134–141

In 1977, my freshman year of high school, there was a statewide contest open to high school art students. The winners would have the honor of painting a horse on the carousel at Quassy Lake Amusement Park in Middlebury, CT. Out of over 1,000 entries from students across the state, I was fortunate to be one of 40 or so selected! The carousel was an original E. Joy Morris, installed at the park around 1908. The Quassy Lake carousel had been the last complete Morris carousel still in operation at the time. Sadly, it was dismantled, and the animals were auctioned off in 1989. This intarsia project is based on the horse I painted all those years ago.

I tackled this project in sections, breaking it down into smaller segments. I cut out and utilized a sacrificial insert to replace the bridle pieces when shaping the horse's head. This allowed me to carve the structure in a fluid shape, with all the pieces where they needed to be in relation to each other without trying to work around the bridle pieces. You will hone your carving skills shaping the muscles in the face and legs. Texturing is added to enhance the blanket trim, tail, and mane. Dying the tassel pieces enhances the spalting of the wood and introduces additional color to the piece.

TOOLS AND MATERIALS

Note: Listed here are the woods I used. I encourage you to get creative and use what you have on hand or can get easily. These wood sizes are only approximate. The size you need can vary greatly depending on how you orient the pattern pieces on the wood. I always recommend having larger pieces to give you more options.

- Maple burl, 15/16"–1" (2.4–2.5cm) thick (for body)
- Figured redwood, 1½" (3.8cm) thick (for saddle)
- Lacewood, 1" (2.5cm) thick (for blanket and collar accents)
- Pupleheart and yellowheart, 15/16"–1" (2.4–2.5cm) thick (for blanket)
- Aromatic red cedar, 15/16"–1" (2.4–2.5cm) thick (for flowers)
- Alaska yellow cedar, 15/16"–1" (2.4–2.5cm) thick (for flowers)
- Green poplar, 15/16"–1" (2.4–2.5cm) thick (for accents)
- Figured walnut, 15/16"–1" (2.4–2.5cm) thick (for mane and tail)
- Spalted red adler, dyed blue, 15/16"–1" (2.4–2.5cm) thick (for tassels)

- Basswood, 15/16"–1" (2.4–2.5cm) thick (for teeth)
- Madrone, 15/16"–1" (2.4–2.5cm) thick (for mouth)
- Ebony, ⅜" (9.5cm) thick (for eye)
- Redheart, 15/16"–1" (2.4–2.5cm) thick (for tassle accents)
- Peruvian walnut, 15/16"–1" (2.4–2.5cm) thick (for hooves)
- Baltic birch plywood, ⅛" (3.2mm) and ¼" (6.4mm); used for risers
- Baltic birch plywood, ¼" x 20" x 25" (6.4 x 508 x 635mm); used for backer
- Blue powder dye (to color tassels)
- Scroll saw
- Scroll saw blades (check instructions for specific sizes)
- Belt sander

- Sanding mop
- Sandpaper, 220 grit
- Sanding sponge or sanding block
- Spindle sander
- Flex drum sander
- Rotary tool and assorted burrs (check instructions for specific types)
- Wood glue
- Skewer
- CA glue
- Utility knife
- Air compressor
- Sharp dental tool
- Rubber-tipped dental tool
- Awl
- Carbon or graphite paper
- L-clamps (however many needed to apply even pressure all over)
- Soft cloths or old socks
- Drill or drill press and assorted bits

- (check instructions for specific sizes)
- Clear packaging tape
- Spray adhesive
- Double-sided tape
- Highlighter
- Scissors
- Pen/pencil
- Waxed paper
- Wood finish (I use a clear gel varnish)
- Paper towels
- Disposable foam or glue brush
- Latex or nitrile gloves
- Black permanent marker
- Rubber bumpers (optional)
- ½" x 25" (1.3 x 63.5cm) leather strip
- 3 x 11 x 5mm brass eye hook
- ⅜" brass jump ring
- Heavy-duty hanger

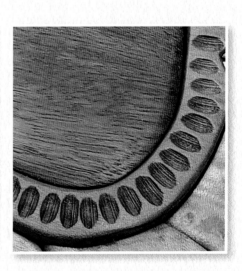

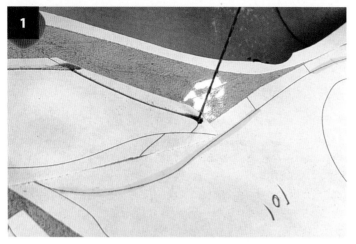

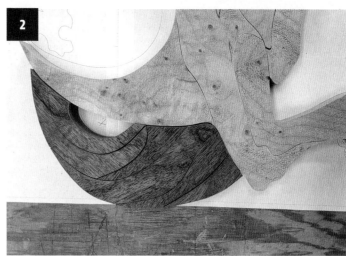

1 **Prepare the pattern and cut the body pieces.** Five copies of the pattern and a master copy will be needed for this project. After your pattern is prepared, cut out the body pieces. When cutting out the larger belly piece, keep the tassel discard piece to reinsert when shaping later. This protects the fragile thinner area of the piece and keeps the shaping consistent.

2 **Cut out the mane and tail.** I used beautifully figured walnut for these areas. Select complementary wood colors for the decorative parts and cut them out.

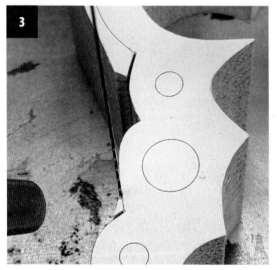

3 **Cut the collar pieces.** When cutting the breast collar pieces, don't make sharp turns. Instead, skip over the *V* areas and come back to them from the other direction to finish the cut.

4 **Test fit your pieces often and adjust as needed.** It's better to get them to fit well now rather than try to figure out where the issue is once all the pieces are cut. If you do have a small fit issue, sand tiny amounts at a time with an oscillating spindle sander, frequently rechecking the fit.

5 **Cut out the eye.** A ⅜" (9.5mm) piece of ebony is used for the eye. It's easier to cut this thickness and add a riser to bring it up to the proper height. The riser thickness needed will depend on the thickness of your wood. In this case, a ½" (1.3cm) riser along with the ⅜" (9.5mm) ebony brought the piece up to the height needed.

6 **Cut the remaining pieces.** Cut out the remaining pieces, then assemble and check the overall fit, making adjustments where necessary.

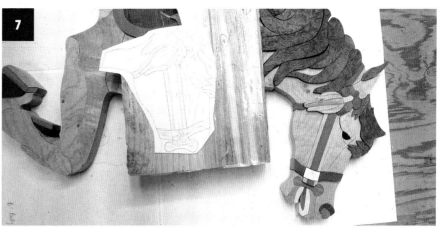

7 **Glue the bridle pieces.** Glue the three main yellow and green bridle pieces together to create one piece. Repeat this with the small yellow-and-green area beside the bit. Because the head is made up of multiple pieces, I needed a way to shape it cohesively. Take an extra copy of the pattern for the bridle and area surrounding the head and cut out a frame, of sorts, from scrap wood to hold the head pieces in place.

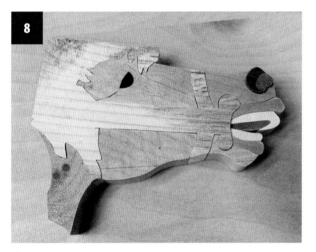

8 **Prepare the head for shaping.** Attach the frame and head pieces to a flat board with double sided turner's tape.

9 **Shape the horse's head.** Using a rotary tool and various power carving bits, rough shape the horse's head. The jaw should be well pronounced, as should the nostril and area around it. Use photo references of horses or carousel horses to get an idea of the areas you want to accentuate. By having the frame piece in place, it allows you to easily carve out the areas you want while keeping everything in place.

10 **Remove scratches and shape the bridle.** Smooth out the scratches of each piece with flex drum sander and fine tune each piece by hand sanding. I used various profile sander attachments with 180-grit sandpaper to go over areas I wanted to enhance. Dry assemble with the bridle pieces. Shape the bridle so that it sits slightly higher than the head. Hand sand to soften the edges of each piece.

11 **Shape the remaining head pieces.** Shape the rest of the head, the mane on the forehead, and the flower. Edge glue the head pieces together (except for the bridle piece that the reins attach to). Assemble next to the unshaped pieces to ensure that the fit and placement is correct. Allow to dry.

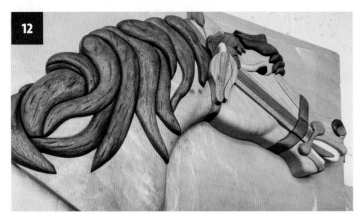

12 **Shape the mane and neck.** Refer to the instructions for the mermaid's hair when shaping the mane (page 54). You want the pieces to flow together. If desired, add some texturing to the mane. When satisfied with your shaping, glue the entire head, neck, and mane pieces together.

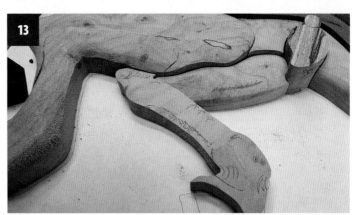

13 **Shape the legs.** Using a scroll saw or band saw, reduce the thickness of the horses left front and left rear leg to roughly ⅝" (1.6cm). They should appear to be behind the primary legs. Carve out muscles and contours. I used many different tools to achieve the look I wanted. Assorted rotary bits, needle files, and profile sander attachments were all utilized. Having reference photos of actual horses or carousel horses is helpful. Refer to photos of the finished project as a reference, as well.

14 **Shape the tail.** Use a sanding shim to shape the overall contour of the tail, then shape the pieces individually. Glue the tail pieces together and shape the rump and belly pieces. Insert the scrap tassel piece into the belly piece before shaping to protect the thin area at the bottom.

15 **Shape the blanket.** The purpleheart/green poplar pieces of the blanket are the same height, roughly ⅛" (3.2mm) higher than the body. Draw a line along the edge of the poplar to reference where the body pieces sit. Mark ⅛" (3.2mm) above this line. Attach the purple and green pieces to a sanding shim and gently sand to the mark. Curve the top slightly to mimic the curve of a horse's body. Separate the pieces. Gently soften both edges of the green band all the way around.

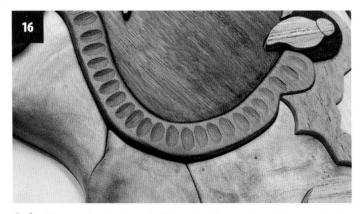

16 **Add texturing (optional).** If desired, add texturing to the green band. I used a Kutzall rotary burr and gently indented all the way around the green strip. The sanding mop softened the marks left by the burr. Always practice texturing on a scrap piece of the same material to get the feel for the burr and what the results will be.

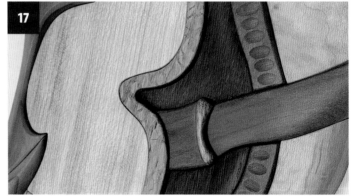

17 **Add risers.** The yellowheart/lacewood section of the blanket is about ⅛" (3.2mm) higher than the purpleheart/poplar segment. I added a ⅛" (3.2mm) riser under this segment to bring up the height. Lightly trace around the edge as you did with the poplar and gently shape, curving upward slightly.

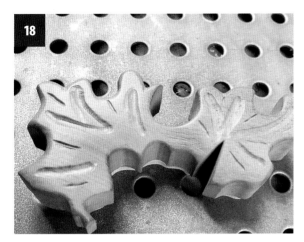

18 **Shape the leaf ornamentation behind the saddle.** The poplar I used here was thinner, so I added a riser first, then carved some vein detail to enhance the look of the leaves. It should sit above the blanket and tuck slightly under the saddle.

19 **Shape the saddle.** The saddle pieces are the thickest. Starting at 1½" (3.8cm) thick, it varies from ½"–⅛" (12.7–3.2mm) thicker than the pieces below. The back segment above the leaf and hibiscus sits the highest, and the main saddle piece is contoured so that it's slightly thinner towards the center—only about ⅛" (3.2mm) higher than the yellow blanket. It is thickest at the front, considerably higher than the breast collar. The entire saddle is curved on an angle to show the shape of the horses back. The girth piece should sit slightly higher than the body and purple/green blanket pieces. It should sit just below the lacewood blanket piece so it appears to go under it.

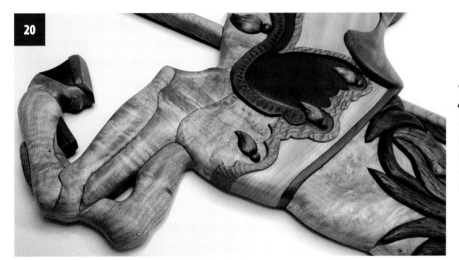

20 **Contour the breast collar pieces.** Contour the breast collar pieces to follow the shape of the neck and shoulders of the horse. The green narrow piece sits slightly higher than the horse's neck. The lacewood piece sits higher than the yellowheart. This adds some extra definition to each of the pieces. They should all follow the same contour.

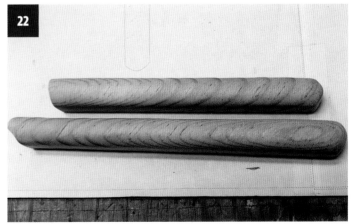

21 **Shape the tassel ornamentation.** These should all sit higher than surrounding pieces to give the look of overlap. Contour one side to give some movement to the pieces.

22 **Shape the upper and lower poles.** Turn the piece side to side while moving it back and forth through the flex drum sander to create an even curve from top to bottom. They should both sit lower than the pieces adjoining them.

23 **Glue the pieces together.** Because of the size of this project, I glued together sections rather than gluing the entire piece. This makes finishing easier. The front legs, back legs, tail and rump, blanket and saddle, breast collar and head are each glued together, respectively. Each segment should be fitted to adjoining areas during the gluing process to ensure a good overall fit. I kept the tassels separate to prevent the stain from bleeding into other pieces. Once the glue has dried, apply painter's tape to all the inside edges. This allows better glue adhesion.

TIP

Staining the Tassels

While this is an optional step, I felt that some extra color fit in with the overall project. Typically, I utilize only the natural colors of the wood. Some say that you shouldn't use stain in intarsia. This is a personal preference. In art, there is no right or wrong. It's your creation to do with as you please. Mixing media, adding color, anything that enhances a piece to you, the artist, is okay. I used Keda dye powder. It is easy to use and can be mixed with water, alcohol, or both. I started with ⅛ tsp of royal blue dye and mixed with 2oz of warm water. I tested the concentration on a scrap piece of the same wood used for the tassels, spalted red alder, to get an idea of how it would look. I applied two thin layers of dye on the tassels and allowed them to dry. The color came out great.

When I put the pieces in place, the color seemed too pronounced to me. So, once the pieces were thoroughly dry, I used the sanding mop to lightly remove some of the dye. I liked the result. The sanding allowed the grain to show through.

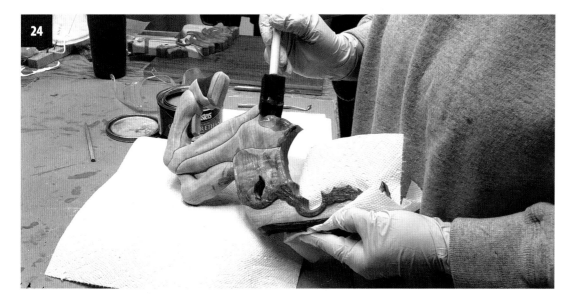

24 **Apply the finish and glue the entire project.** Complete each segment before moving on to the next, saving the stained pieces for last. You want to have time to remove all the excess finish before it dries. Remove the painter's tape and glue the entire project together. I left the piece that the reins would be attached to unglued for now to make assembly of the reins easier.

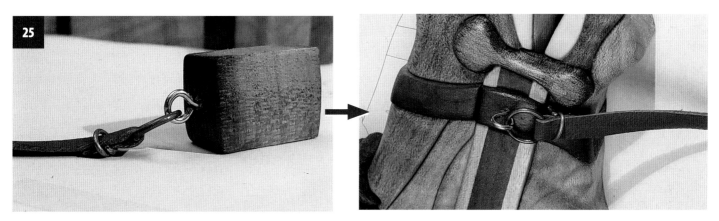

25 **Make the reins.** I ordered several ½"-wide, 25"-long (1.3 x 63.5cm) pieces of thin, soft leather. I wasn't sure what color I'd want, so I picked several to have options. Once the project was completed, I decided that ¼" (6.4mm) wide reins worked better. I repurposed a ⅜" (9.5mm) jump ring and a brass link from an old necklace and used a size 3 x 11 x 5mm brass eye hook. Loop ⅜" (9.5mm) of the rein through the ring and apply a small dab of CA glue gel to seal the loop. Open the eye hook slightly with small needle nose pliers and loop the ring through. Close the eye hook and screw it into the center of the wood bridle piece so that the eye hook ends up sitting vertically. Slide the metal link piece through the reins until it sits over the looped part. If needed, trim to size with pliers so that the ends are hidden behind the reins. Insert the wood piece back into the bridle. To get the desired length of the reins, drape the reins loosely over the top pole, looping around it once. Cut off approximately 6" (15.2cm) to use for the inside rein. Remove the bridle piece and reins and set them aside to glue into place once the backer has been attached.

26 **Make the backer and affix the hanger.** Make your backer following the usual steps and glue the project to it. Be sure to use a sturdy hanger! Make sure to include the two inside holes that will be cut out at the tail and between the two front legs. Cut out the backer with a #3 blade.

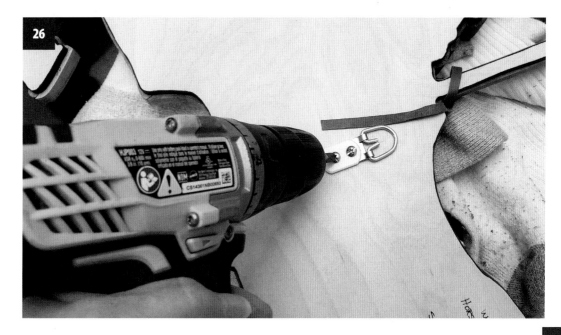

All patterns should be copied at 100% size.

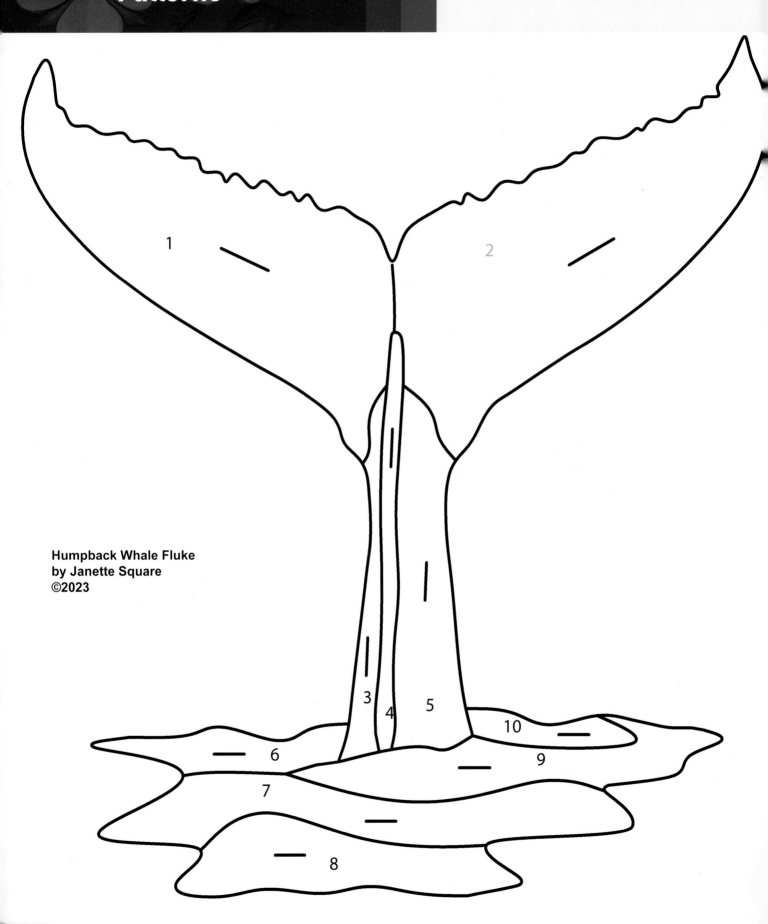

Humpback Whale Fluke
by Janette Square
©2023

Sports Car Intarsia
Designed by Janette Square
©2023

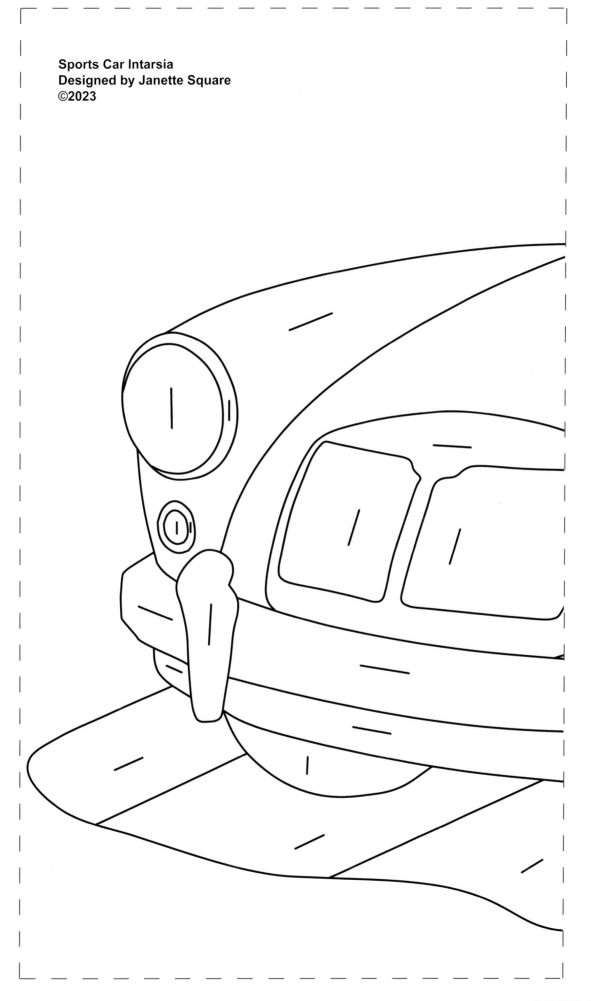

INTARSIA WOODWORKING MADE EASY

Intarsia Mermaid
Designed by Janette Square
©2023

23

24

Succulent Intarsia Pattern
Designed by Janette Square
©2023

Fish Magnet
Intarsia Pattern
Designed by Janette Square
©2023

INTARSIA WOODWORKING MADE EASY

Dogwood Branches
Intarsia Pattern
Designed by Janette Square
©2023

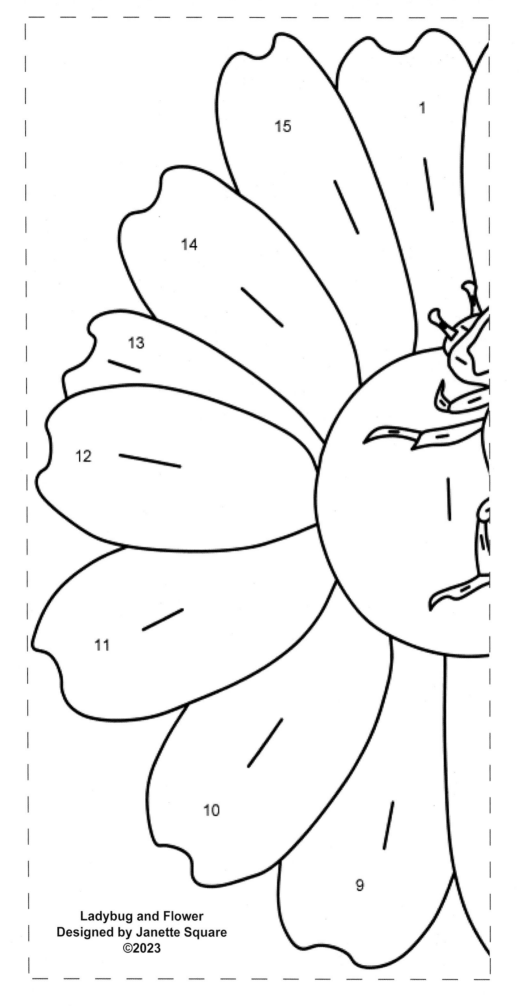

Ladybug and Flower
Designed by Janette Square
©2023

Wood Duck on a Branch
Intarsia Pattern
Designed by Janette Square
©2023

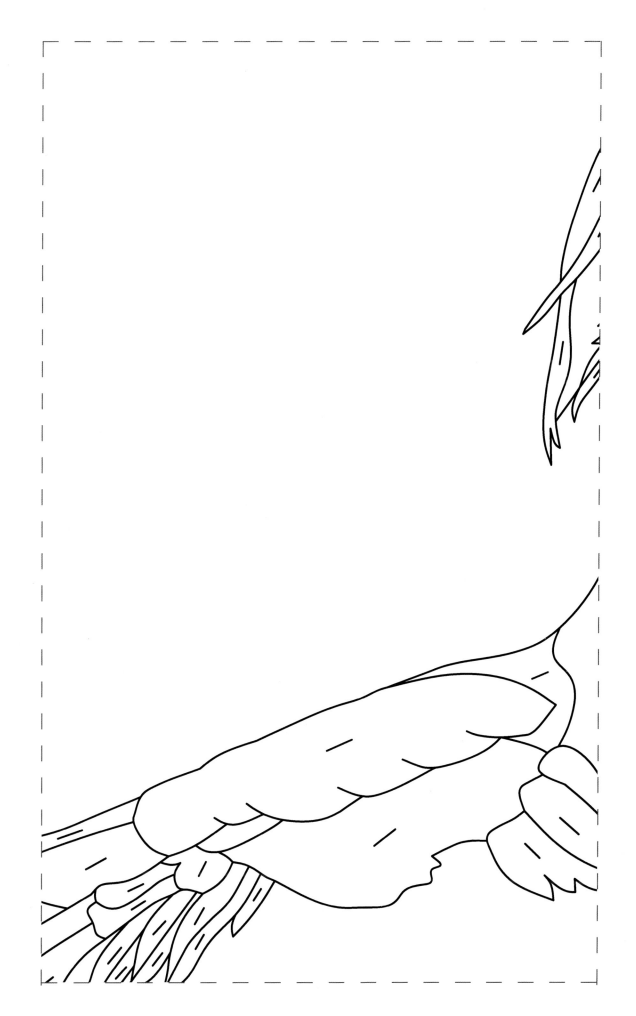

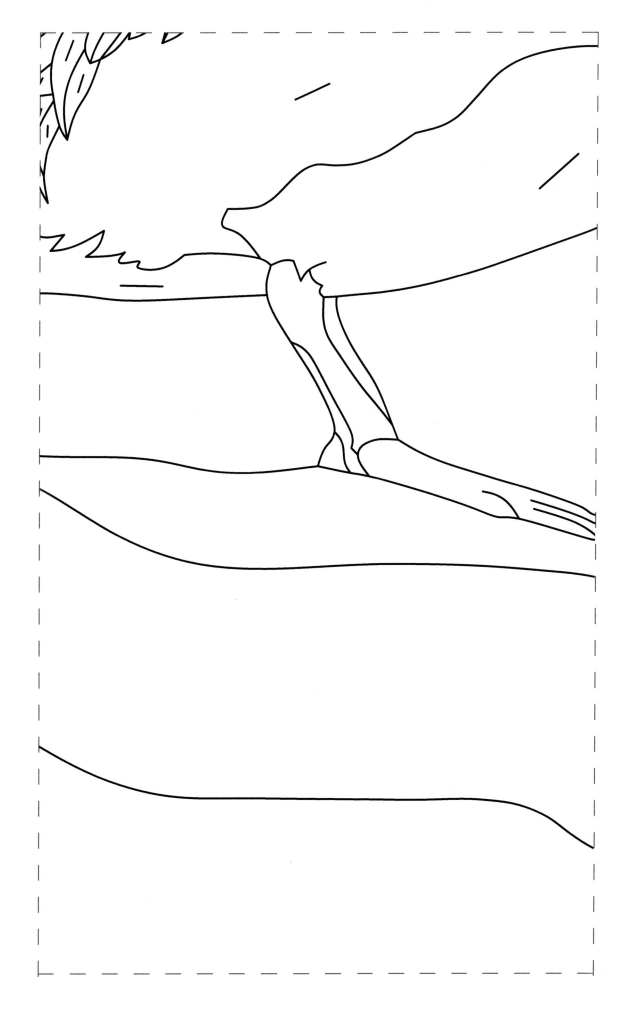

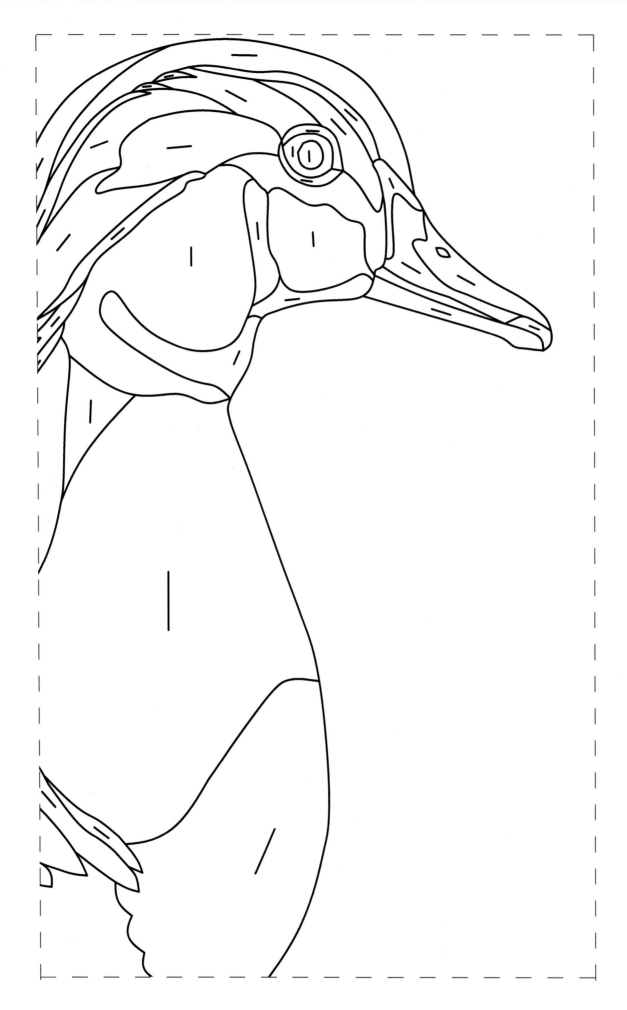

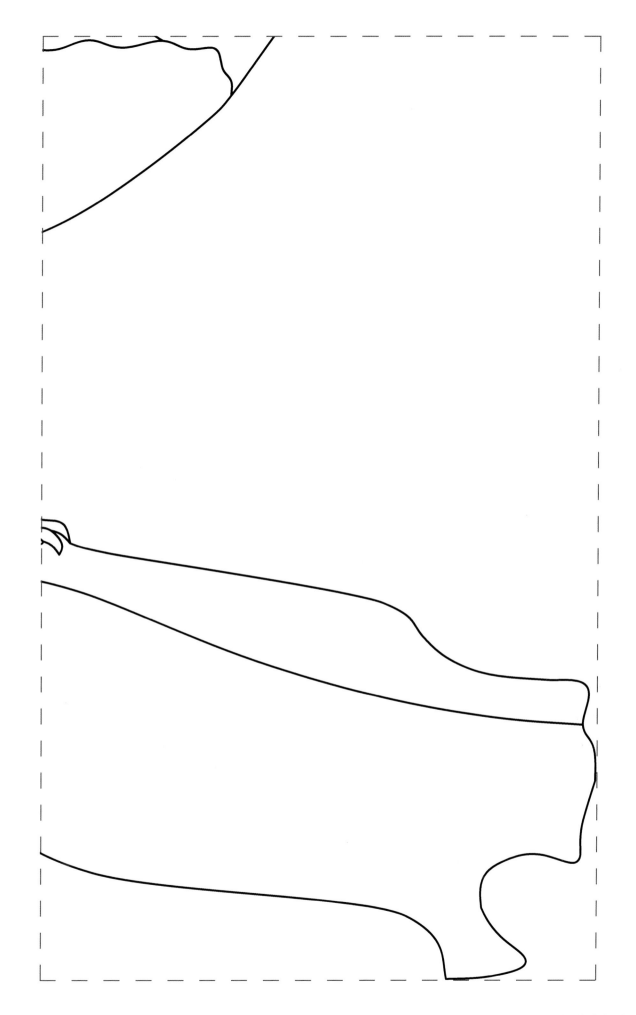

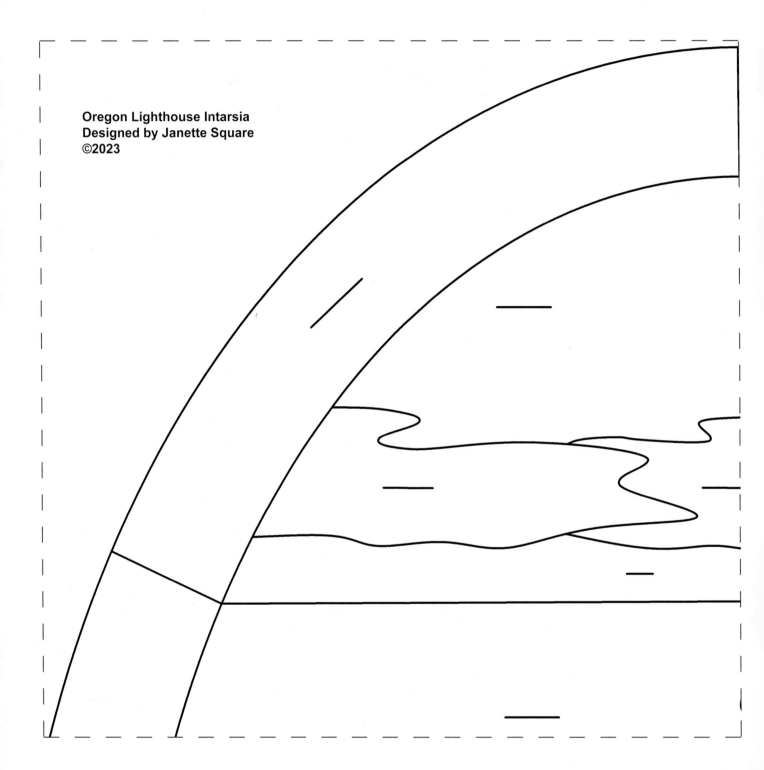

Oregon Lighthouse Intarsia
Designed by Janette Square
©2023

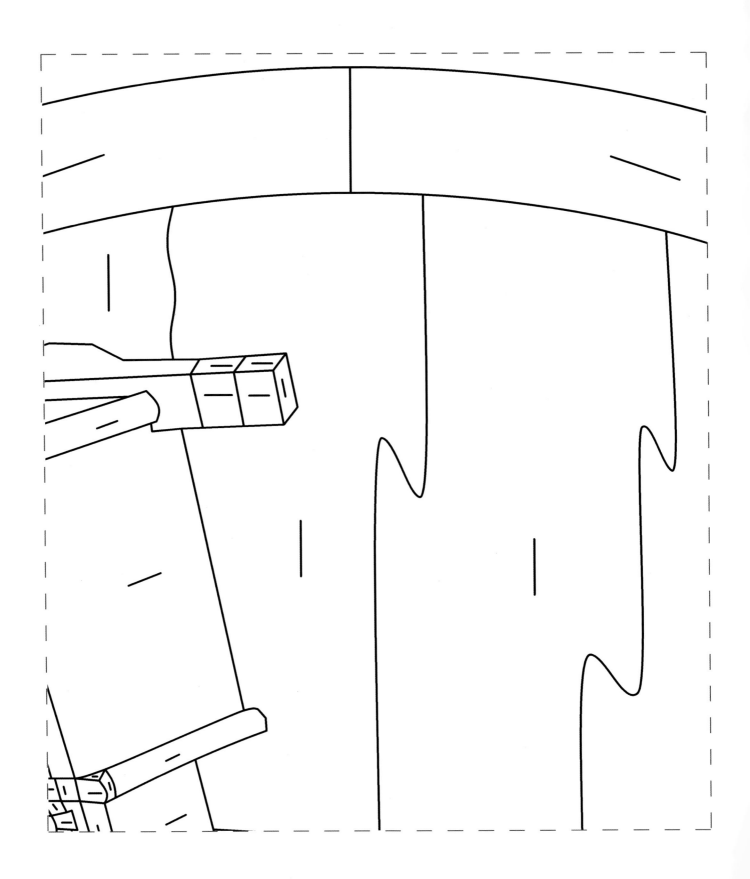

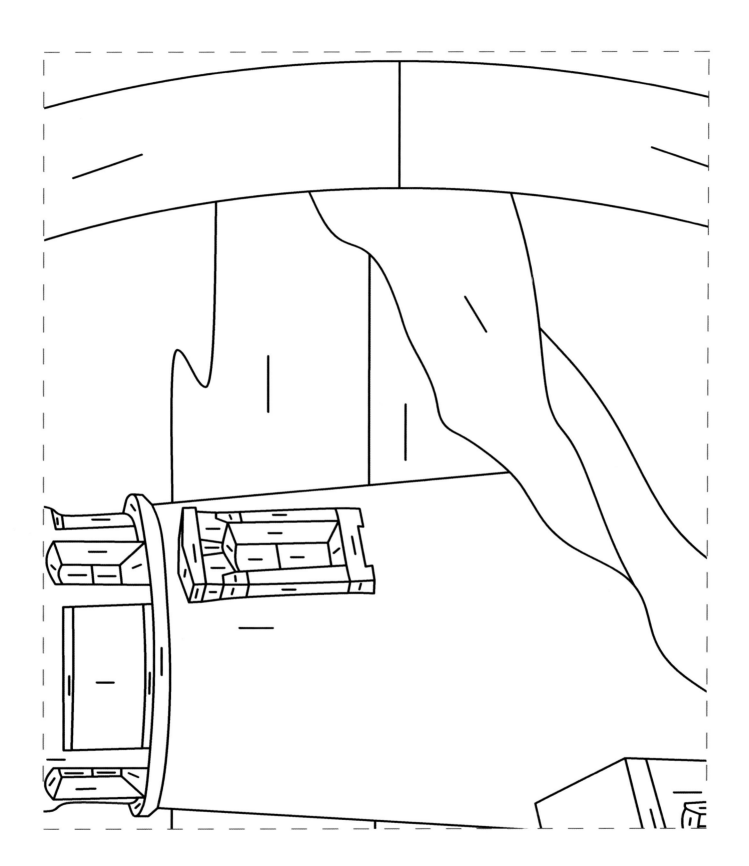

INTARSIA WOODWORKING MADE EASY

E. Joy Morris Style
Carousel Horse
Designed by Janette Square
©2023

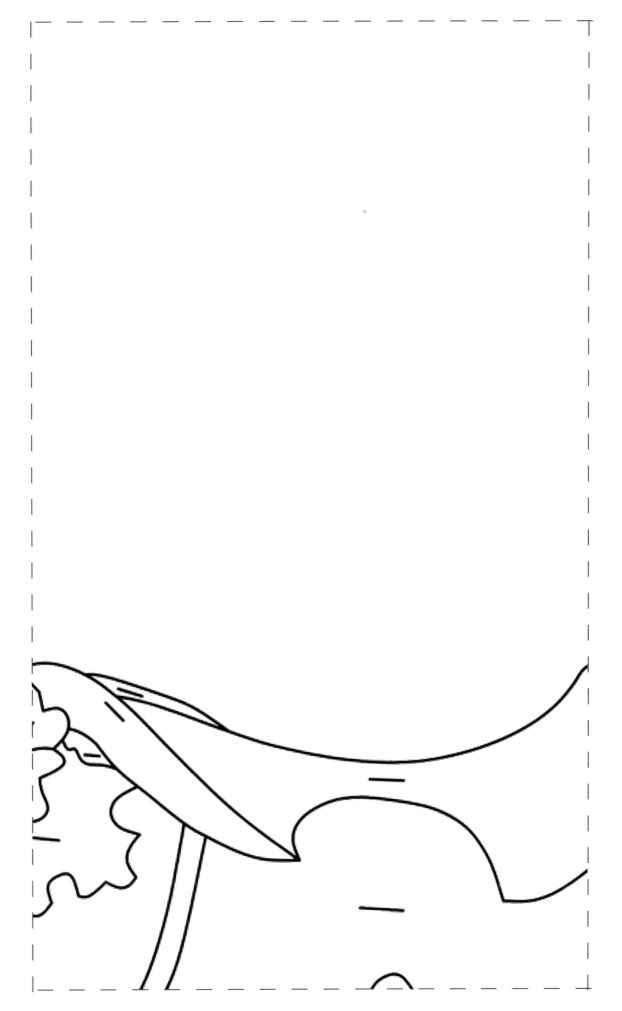

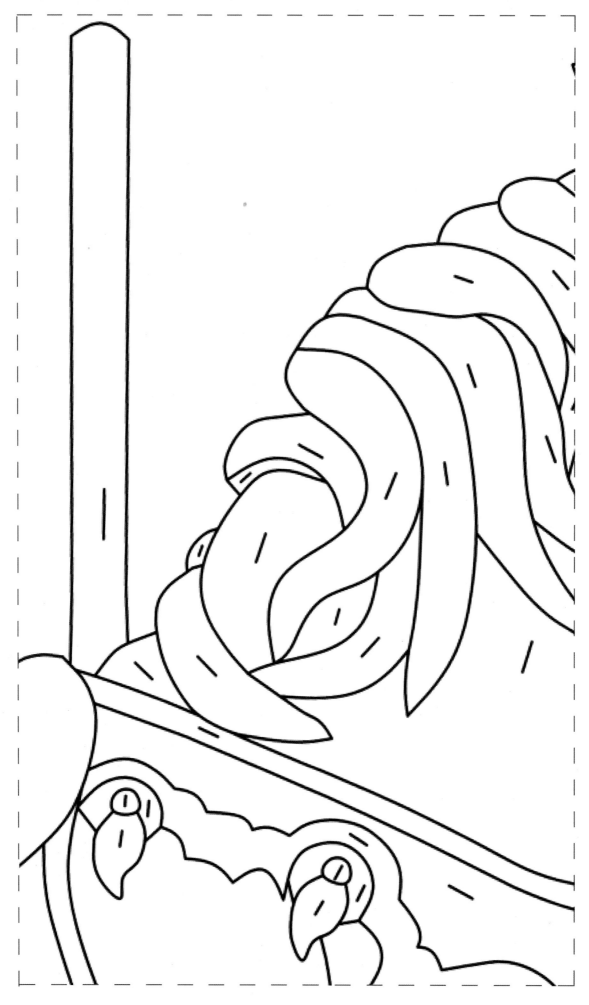

INTARSIA WOODWORKING MADE EASY

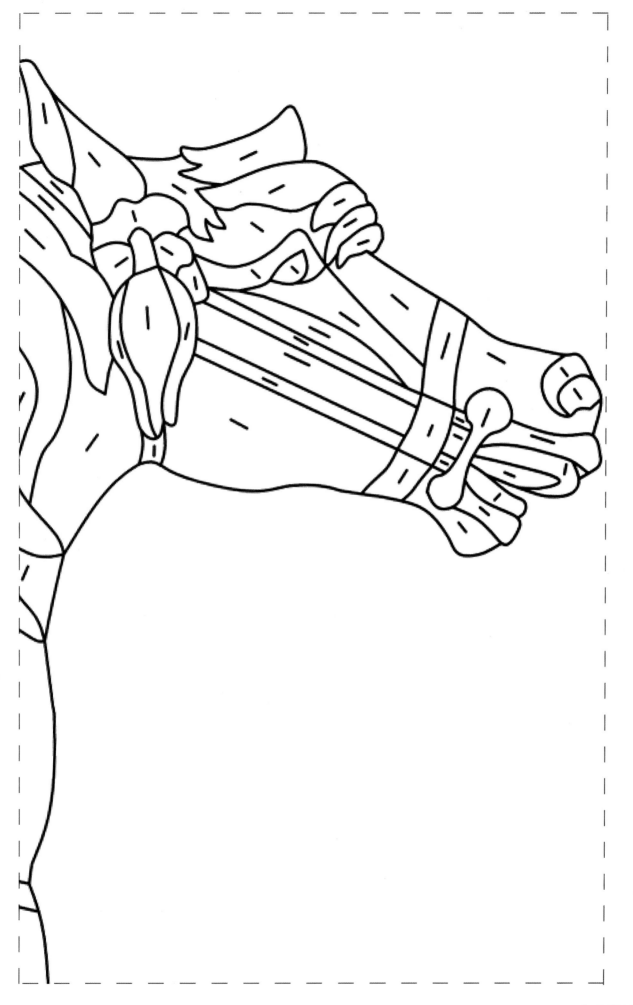

INTARSIA WOODWORKING MADE EASY

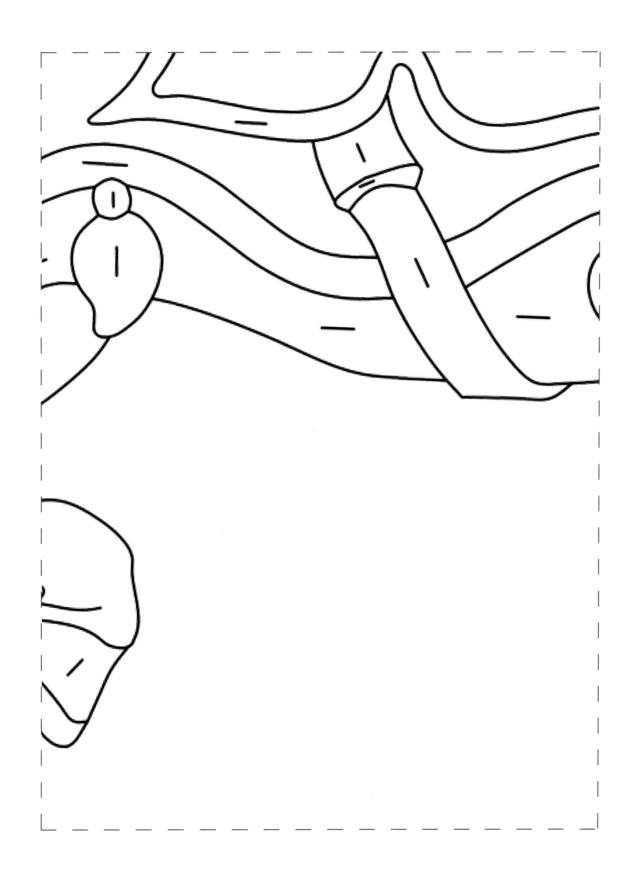

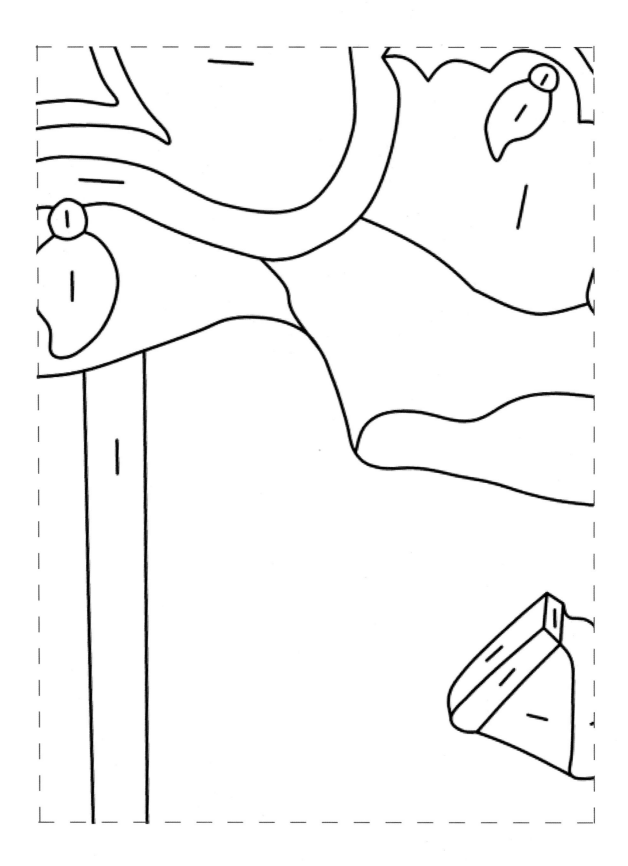

INTARSIA WOODWORKING MADE EASY

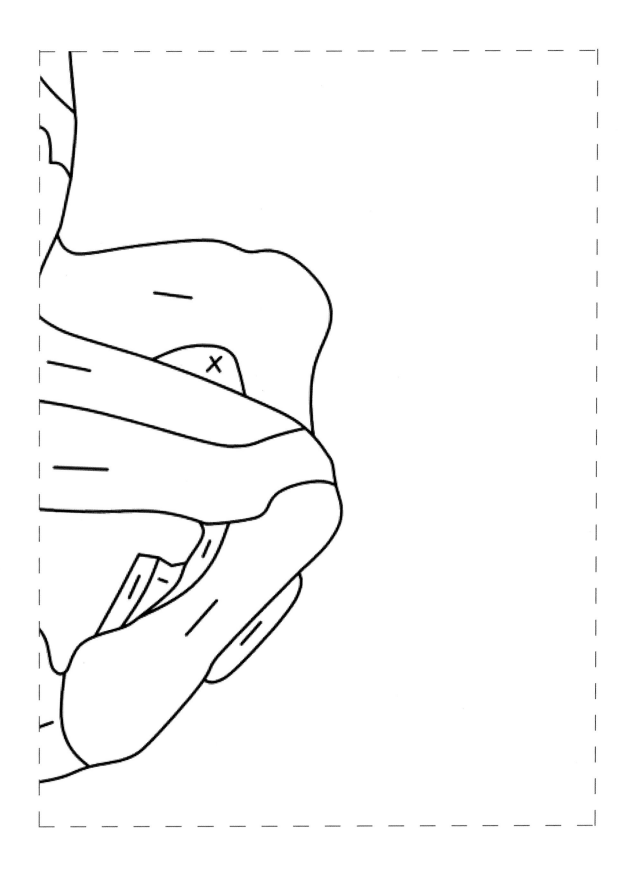

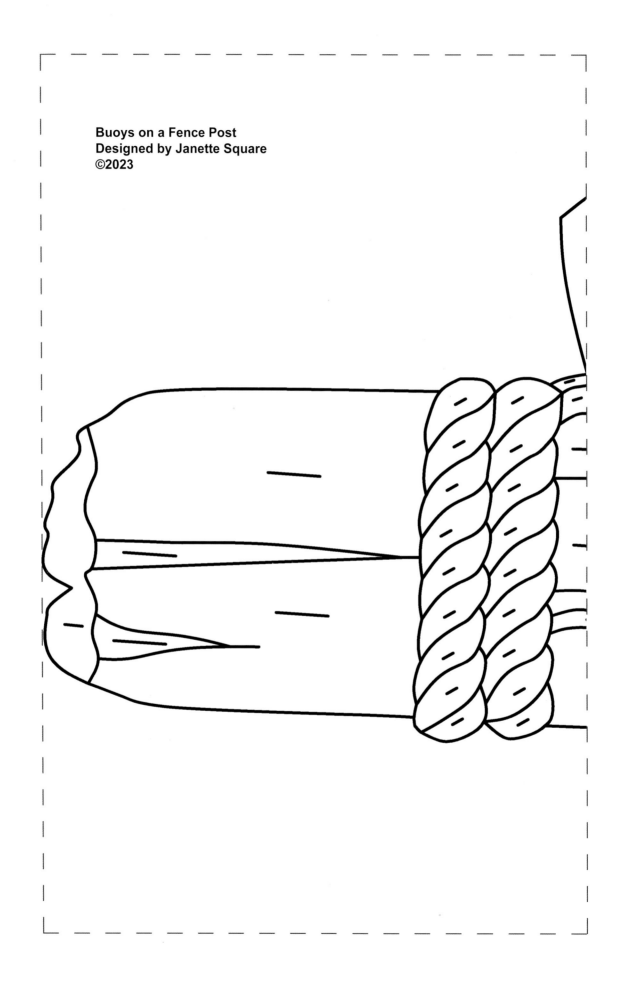

Buoys on a Fence Post
Designed by Janette Square
©2023

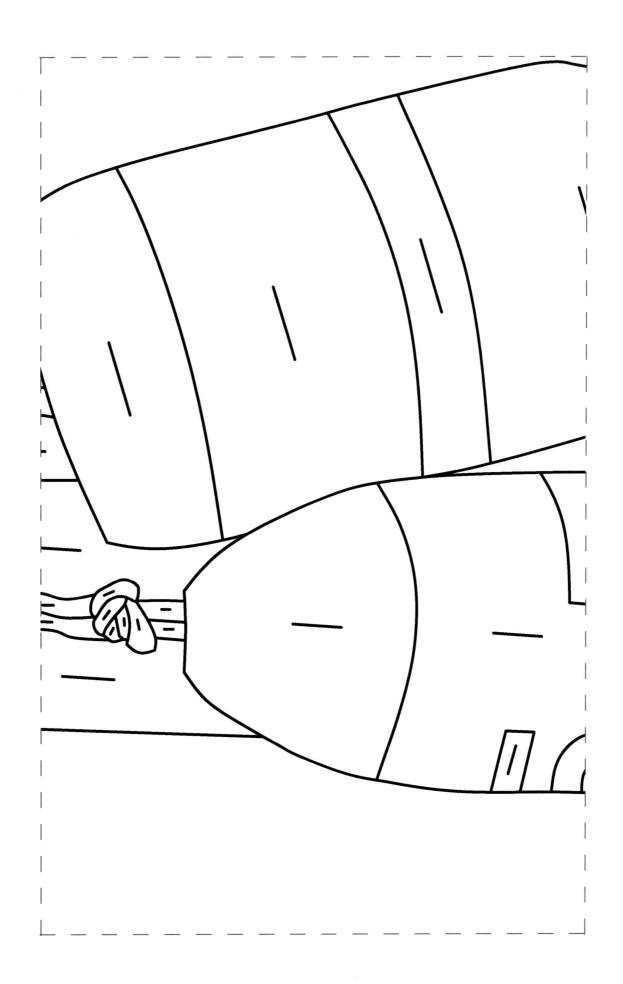

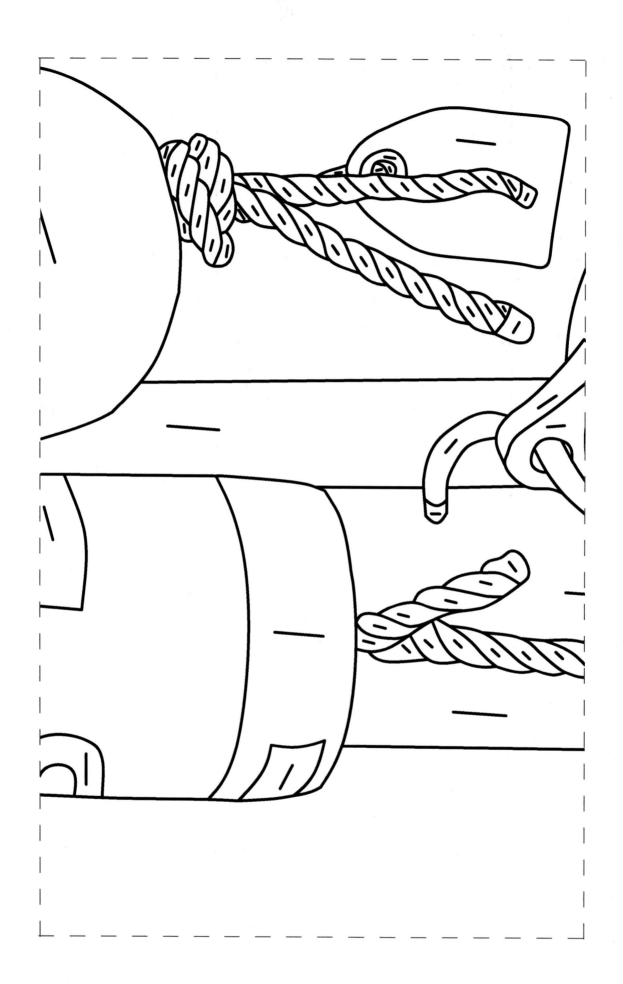

INTARSIA WOODWORKING MADE EASY

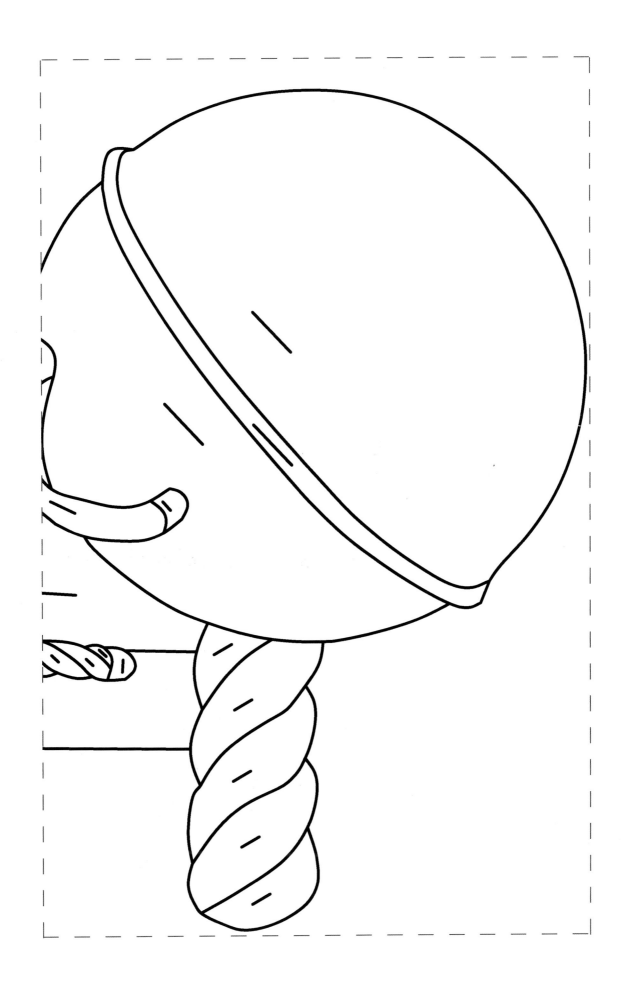

Index

A

African mahogany, 54
air compressor, 19
Alaska yellow cedar, 102
alder, 54; red, 25; spalted red, 46
aspen, 12, 22, 23, 46, 62, 70, 82, 88, 96
awl, 10, 20, 21

B

backer: affixing project to, 20; clamping, 21; making, 20; options, 52; using permanent marker on edges, 20
ball burr, 50–51
Baltic birch plywood, 38, 46, 52, 62, 70, 82, 88, 102
Bartley's Gel Varnish, 19
basswood, 102
belt sander, 9, 15; tip, 52, 56
blades, for scroll saw, 7–8; checking squareness of, 15–16; preparing, 15; tip for cutting, 16, 31, 40, 41, 48, 49
blue painter's tape, 10, 101
blue pine, 22, 28, 82, 88
brad point bit, 72
buckeye burl, 23, 96
buffing, 17, 33
butternut, 25, 46, 54

C

CA (cyanoacrylate) gel glue, 18; using with spalted wood, 26
camphor burl, 38

cedar, 12, 76; Alaska yellow, 102; red, 22, 23, 25, 46, 70, 82, 88, 102
cherry, 23
clamps: assorted, 10; L-, 38; using to attach backer, 21
coloring options beyond wood, 27; dyes, 98; staining, 108
contour: adding, 24; creating depth and, 24
curly maple, 23, 82, 96
cut-and-paste method for pattern transfer, 13
cutting wood, tips for, 16, 31, 40, 41, 48, 49
cyanoacrylate (CA) gel glue, 18; using with spalted wood, 26

D

Danish oil, 19
dental tools, sharp-tipped and rubber-tipped, 10; using, 19
depth, creating , 22; contours and, 24
drill bit gauge, 10
drill press with flex drum sander attachment, 8
drum sander: flex, attachment, 8; inflatable, 8
dust collection, 6; system, 10
dust mask, 10
dyes, practicing with, 98; tip, 100

E

ebonizing, 27
ebony, 23, 96, 102
embellishments, 27
eraser, 10

Index

Photo Credits

About the Author

I've always been creative in some form. Until intarsia, my outlets were drawing, photography, gardening, and creating pressed flower bouquets. In 1995, my husband and I—along with our three cats— moved to Eugene, Oregon from Toronto, Canada. Here, I first discovered intarsia at a local craft show. I was fascinated. We purchased pieces for ourselves and as gifts. These were all created from Western red cedar. Around 1999, Kevin, my husband, became interested in woodworking and began accumulating tools. Looking for an excuse to spend time in the shop, I bought a scroll saw and began exploring how this interesting art form called intarsia was created. Armed with a book by Judy Gayle Roberts, a few blades, and some wood, I made the first two projects from Judy's book. I was hooked! My first visit to a lumber store was an eye opener; there were so many varieties and colors of wood! I was amazed at the beautiful choices. Why only use one type of wood when you can use several? I purchased more patterns, and my wood addiction began.

In December 2002, I found myself unemployed, and by the following June, I was doing my first Arts & Crafts show and creating intarsia full time. Being a cat person, I gravitated toward cat designs. Not finding many that had the realism I was looking for, I began designing my own. Then and still, I lean toward designing detailed, realistic projects, especially portraits of beloved furry companions. In 2005, I received honorable mention in *Scroll Saw Woodworking & Crafts's design* contest challenge with a portrait I created of a ragdoll cat. Shortly thereafter, I became a contributor to the magazine. I was becoming known for my custom pet portraits, and since then, have memorialized pets in wood for clients all over the world. One of these portraits, "Tailgate Party," won Best in Show and People's Choice Award at the Rhododendron Festival in Florence, OR. Throughout my career, I've been featured in numerous publications and even local TV news. I have been contributing to *Scroll Saw Woodworking & Crafts* and other magazines since 2006. I also enjoy giving private classes to aspiring intarsia artists. In 2014, I took this to the next level by giving seminars at the Fine Woodworking Showcase in Saratoga Springs, NY and the Fox Chapel Woodworking Show in PA. I felt like a rock star at these events and would love to do more in the future! Meeting intarsia enthusiasts and helping them to become better at the craft we all love is very rewarding.

These days, I reside in a small village on the central Oregon Coast with my husband and varying number of cats. I do my best to keep my tools from rusting from the salt air and gather much of my design inspiration from the beauty of nature that surrounds me in this very special corner of the world.

Janette